The Point

PRAISE FOR *THE POINT*

"You might say that communication is the root of all good and the root of all evil. If you are trying to accomplish the former and avoid the latter, *The Point* takes you down the path.

Written in an easy-to-digest style and packed with quotes, rules-of-thumb and examples for everyone to follow, *The Point* is a must for every individual professional and business team alike. Whether you need more efficiency or efficacy from your emails, presentations, collaborations, social media posts, networking or anything else, *The Point* is your bible. Get *The Point*, get to the point and get more out of your work."

> **-Carol Roth**, "Recovering" Investment Banker, best-selling
> Author, TV Pundit and Business Consigliere

"No business can succeed without effective leadership. And no leader can succeed without constantly improving his or her communication skills. Steve Woodruff is the guru of clarity, and *The Point* is the fruit of his decades of devotion learning the craft of clear communications. Read Steve's book, and you'll become a better communicator and leader beginning with your next email."

> **-Kevin Kruse**, CEO and Founder, LEADx and
> *New York Times* Best-Selling author

"*The Point* is a comprehensive MBA on communication skills, perhaps the most overlooked skill set in most corporate leadership curriculums. Any wonder that the annual employee survey always lists communication as the number one area for improvement. Should be required reading for leaders and individual contributors."

> **-John Hoskins**, Author and Founder of Level Five Selling

"If you want people to listen, then get right to the point. This little book is crammed full of the essential tips you need to do that. I sure wish everybody who was wasting my precious time would read *The Point* first!"

> **-Josh Bernoff**, best-selling author of
> *Build a Better Business Book*

"Steve Woodruff does with *The Point* what I wish more people did with their own communication: he gets right to...wait for it...the point."

-**Chris Brogan**, *New York Times* Best-Selling author

"Victory goes to the best communicator. If you seek to win in work and at life, master the craft of clarity by immersing yourself in Steve Woodruff's book, *The Point*."

-**Michael Stelzner**, founder and CEO of
Social Media Examiner

"Clarity is key to being successful in sales. No clarity - no sales. When I think of getting clarity in my sales messaging, I think of Steve Woodruff. The Clarity Fuel Formula has helped me have better conversations - and make more sales - many times over the years."

-**Phil Gerbyshak**, author of *Zero Dollar Consultancy*

"Steve is my personal clarity guru, and his book is a gift to the world!"

-**Mark W. Schaefer**, Executive Director, Schaefer Marketing
Solutions and best-selling author of *Belonging to the Brand*

"The listeners of my podcast loved hearing from Steve after his first book (Clarity Wins), and I found immediate value applying his insights and suggestions. I expect even greater things from *The Point*. A universal formula for clear communications? How can anyone not love that?"

-**Jeff Brown**, author, speaker, and
podcast host at *Read to Lead*

"When I wanted to train my team of marketers on improved communication skills, I turned to the King of Clarity himself, Steve Woodruff. And he delivered. Steve's book outlines all the principles and practices that continue to make a huge difference in our work. *The Point* has my highest recommendation."

-**Steph Dreyer**, Marketing Director, MetLife and Vice Chair,
Board of Directors, The LAM Foundation

"Working with Steve accelerated our growth curve tenfold. Using Steve's clarity insights and principles helped us to laser-focus our message, moving beyond the "how" we do things to the "why" and the customer WIIFM (What's In It For Me)."

-**Ed McCarthy**, CEO, Echelon Performance

"In today's noisy business world, it's more important than ever to be clear and concise in your communication. Steve Woodruff's Clarity Fuel Formula is a great resource for anyone who wants to improve their communication skills. Steve has a simple but effective framework for creating clear, concise, and persuasive messages. It has helped me and my team, and I highly recommend *The Point* to anyone who wants to be a more effective communicator."

-**John Sjovall**, Executive Director, Commercial Learning & Development, SK Life Science, Inc.

"As my coach, Steve played a key role in bringing clarity to how I was going to make a significant transition in my career. He has a special talent for taking what seems complex down to the clear and simple - whether that's in his coaching practice, facilitating workshops or writing. I will forever be grateful for his help in getting me out of "my box" and guiding me to pursue my passion and work that I love."

-**Kari Gearhart**, Principal, The Performance Bridge, and author, *REACH – Using Fitness to Grow Your Leadership*

"Clarity is something my career coaching clients struggle with - what career path they desire, how they wish to be challenged, who they are and what they bring to the table. Steve's ability to make this narrative simple, clear, concise and to *The Point* has been a game changer for them."

-**Andrea H. Pagnozzi**, Principal, Flint Coaching and Consulting LLC

"Don't you wish people would 'get to the point'? If everyone would read *The Point*, they would. Steve's work on clarity and getting to *The Point* helps people of all walks of life be better thinkers and communicators."

-**Jeff Gaus**, CEO, The Provenance Chain™ Network

"In a world full of content noise and information churn, there is one thing that will connect your message with your audience - clarity. Steve Woodruff, the King of Clarity, will show you how to distill your message down to the essence that cuts through jargon and fluff and gets right to *The Point*."

-**Catherine Altman Morgan**, career transition expert and author of *This Isn't Working!*

"Newsflash: Humans don't suffer from shorter attention spans. We just have less time to pay attention, and more noise to distract us. That's why successful professionals will buy *The Point* and learn to master the art of communication clarity."

-**Tom Martin**, President of Converse Digital and author of *The Invisible Sale*

"In my various professional roles since first meeting Steve, I have found his clarity principles applicable to everything: training, leadership, conversations, marketing, and branding. *The Point* will be an outstanding resource for every professional who needs to make an impact in meetings, emails, and pitches. Don't be pointless. Learn to sharpen your skills and communicate with *The Point*!"

-**Carrie Schaal**, Senior Vice President of Business Development, Educational Resource Systems Inc.

"Steve Woodruff's insight and clarity in communicating and branding has been nothing short of invaluable to me as a small business owner. In a world of oversaturation, being able to bring clarity and focus to your message is absolutely critical. And Steve delivers just that!"

-**Sarah Brown**, Creator and Owner of Math Songs

"The hardest job for every leader is to be clear. People won't trust what is not clear. Leaders who are clear are trusted. Steve is a master at clarity; I know from personal experience working with Steve, and I know you're going to find amazing value in *The Point*."

-Gerry Edtl, Partner, Gerry Edtl Consulting, LLC

"Prepare to embark on a journey of self-discovery and transformation as you gain clarity. Steve and his work are an indispensable resource for anyone seeking to communicate effectively, inspire others, and leave a lasting impact."

-Christy Soukhamnuet, Managing Director,
Texas Capital Bank

"I launched my current company, ROCK Creative Network and in the beginning years, struggled to articulate the purpose for which I was called in starting this new venture. Steve provided strategic clarity and messaging that I use to this day. I promise you: light bulbs will come on bright as you read about Steve's Clarity Fuel Formula in *The Point*."

-George Weyrauch II, Founder, ROCK Creative Network

"The ability to communicate with precision and conciseness can make all the difference in capturing attention, inspiring action, and driving results. That's why I turn to Steve Woodruff as the go-to resource for unlocking the power of clear and impactful communication. To achieve clarity in your business communications, look no further than Steve Woodruff's new book, *The Point*."

-Lola Gershfield, PsyD, CEO of EmC Leaders, Inc.

"Steve is the reigning 'King of Clarity'. His philosophy surrounding saying what you mean – in a clear, concise and meaningful way, without gibberish and extra fluff – is exactly what we all need in our soundbite, scrolling world today. Steve led my small-business team in a Clarity workshop based on his formula, helping us gain the focus we needed for growth and success."

-Kim Catania, Principal, Catania Communications

The
Point

HOW TO WIN WITH
CLARITY-FUELED COMMUNICATIONS

Steve Woodruff

NEW YORK

LONDON • NASHVILLE • MELBOURNE • VANCOUVER

The Point

HOW TO WIN WITH CLARITY-FUELED COMMUNICATIONS

© 2024 Steve Woodruff

Published in New York, New York, by Morgan James Publishing. Morgan James is a trademark of Morgan James, LLC. www.MorganJamesPublishing.com

Proudly distributed by Publishers Group West®

A **FREE** ebook edition is available for you
or a friend with the purchase of this print book.

CLEARLY SIGN YOUR NAME ABOVE

Instructions to claim your free ebook edition:
1. Visit MorganJamesBOGO.com
2. Sign your name CLEARLY in the space above
3. Complete the form and submit a photo
   of this entire page
4. You or your friend can download the ebook
   to your preferred device

ISBN 9781636982380 paperback
ISBN 9781636982397 ebook
Library of Congress Control Number:
2023939047

Cover and Interior Design by:
Chris Treccani
www.3dogcreative.net

Graphics by:
Olivia Blandin
olivianoelcreative.com

Edited by:
Josh Bernoff (content)
Merlina McGovern (copy)

Morgan James is a proud partner of Habitat for Humanity Peninsula
and Greater Williamsburg. Partners in building since 2006.

Get involved today! Visit: www.morgan-james-publishing.com/giving-back

To my dear wife, Sandy Woodruff. You have been my coconspirator and best friend for more than four decades and an anchor of unwavering love and support for me, our five boys, your students, and countless others.

Plus—you're the world's best "combobulator"!

TABLE OF CONTENTS

FOREWORD

The words seemed weird, for sure.

"We built this city. We built this city on sausage rolls."

But, like many others in the 1980s, I happily sang along with this misheard lyric from the rock group Jefferson Starship. Hey—I've got no beef with sausage rolls.

However, the real lyrics are, "We built this city on rock and roll." Oops. Even a catchy chorus can be misunderstood. Just sprinkle a bit of bad enunciation over a tortured metaphor and you've got a recipe for confusion.

Decades later, it seems like clarity is getting worse, doesn't it? From emojis to chatbots. From Gen Z slang to business jargon. From customer service departments to government leaders. Why is it so hard to just say or write what we mean?

Thankfully, Steve Woodruff is here to help.

I've known Steve for more than a dozen years, and his ability to understand the root causes of clarity deficits is unmatched, period.

But, more importantly, he knows exactly how to solve these common problems. His Clarity Fuel Formula approach will make you a more effective communicator in every aspect of your life.

And who doesn't want that?

Because when you really step back and ponder it (put on a little Jefferson Starship, pour yourself a nice tequila, and give this a think), aren't many of our problems in life and business created by lack of clarity?

Argument with spouse? Probably a clarity and communication issue.

Miscommunication with a colleague? Somebody didn't describe what they needed well enough.

Miffed at a friend? Tried not to hurt her feelings, and thus wasn't clear, and now made it worse.

Clarity deficits are EVERYWHERE. And they can be much more costly than a sausage roll.

Once you complete this exceedingly practical and useful book, you'll not only recognize clarity problems emerging in advance (a very handy skill), you'll also be able to rectify them using Steve's winning techniques.

A friend asked me a while back who I thought would benefit from Steve Woodruff's work on clarity and communication. I thought a moment and provided a truly honest answer:

"Only people with mouths and/or keyboards."

If that's you, you're going to love this book. It's brief, to the point, and absolutely loaded with actionable takeaways.

I'm a professional communicator in the written word, audio, video, and public speaking. And I still learn something new every single time I sip from the cup of Steve's genius.

No, not "sippy cup." That's for babies. See how easy it is to miss the mark on clarity?

Enjoy *The Point!*

-**Jay Baer**—*New York Times* best-selling author and member of the Professional Speaking Hall of Fame.

INTRODUCTION

I t looks so easy, this whole communication thing.
Message delivered. Message received. Success! If only...

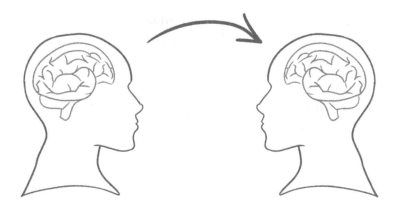

This book would end right here on the first page if things were that simple. But sixty-plus years of living in the real world has convinced me that effective communication is one of the biggest challenges we all face.

And I mean *all* of us. 8+ billion human beings.

We see miscommunication all the time in life's mundane exchanges. "Would you like fries with that?" asks the person at the fast-food drive-through. As you drive away, you realize you ended up with onion rings, not French fries. Now, I'd personally consider that an upgrade, but still, the message didn't make it all the way across the finish line.

The purpose of communication isn't just pushing out words; it's really all about achieving an intended result. Our words are tools, and we want to use them skillfully to accomplish specific goals.

Imagine us watching a typical business presentation. We're sitting restlessly in the audience while a speaker drones through a fogbank of statistics and graphs and jumbled sentences. Blah-blah-bullet point, blah-blah-bullet point. The speaker clearly believes that no detail should be left behind.

"Just get to the point!" rattles through your mind as you begin plotting your escape. Finally, you turn to a much more interesting alternative: your smartphone.

This is a lost opportunity for the speaker—and for the listener. The speaker's intended result of this encounter was to enlighten, not overwhelm. But TMI (Too Much Information) has defeated the purpose. We have become the latest victims of "death by PowerPoint."

In a world full of increasing noise, less is more. Simplicity and brevity win, verbosity and vagueness lose. Lincoln's Gettysburg Address was less than two minutes long. The speech by top-shelf orator Edward Everett that preceded it: two hours. Which one do you remember?

Of course, speakers and presenters aren't the only ones that lose their audiences. Think of meandering meetings. Never-ending conference calls. Confusing emails. Droning sermons. Information poorly delivered is information rarely received.

Since we all live and work in a busy and distracting environment, nobody has the time and energy to figure out the relevant point of your communication. Your most direct path to winning the war for attention and comprehension is to use words that work. The fewer the better. Your audience wants the needle, not another haystack. Clarity, not confusion.

I wrote this book so you can win at the most important competition of all: getting your point across and accomplishing your purpose. In every sphere of life.

As you begin the journey, here's my *promise*: By skillfully and consistently applying the simple tactics of the Clarity Fuel Formula, you will become an increasingly effective communicator.

And here's my *premise*: The most direct route to successful communication is to package your messages in what I call "brain-friendly" formats, a skill anyone can learn and apply.

But there are barriers to getting our ideas across to others, so let's begin by finding out what is in our way.

Part 1:

Our Formidable Communication Challenges

Your every attempt at communication is launched into a busy, buzzing environment of hubbub and distraction.

It takes no skill to generate words. Millions of them are being generated and tossed out into the world at this very moment. But getting heard and understood? That's a huge challenge. In fact, you're facing that challenge on two fronts: external (the environment) and internal (the mind of your audience).

What are your primary hurdles?

- A loud chorus of other voices and inputs, which threatens to drown out your message; and

- A processing system (the human brain) that is extremely picky about what it will receive and remember.

Anyone can speak. Few get heard. As you'll soon discover, the signal-to-noise ratio is frightening. Your audience's brains are filtering out exponentially more than they let in.

You must fight through some serious opposition for every inch of mindshare you gain.

It's trench warfare out there in our noisy, boisterous world. Every day, your audience is barraged by figurative dump trucks spilling out piles of words at their front doors. Your daily challenge, and mine, is to figure out how to break through and rise above the noise.

Clarity will help you win this battle. And I'm going to hand you the best weapons I've found. But first, exactly why is it so difficult to be heard and understood? How do these hurdles get in our way?

CHAPTER 1:

The Barriers

Sun Tzu famously said, "Know the enemy." To win in the communications battle, you first need to understand what you're up against.

Any successful coach prepares her team by getting very specific about this week's opponent. This player. That formation. This weakness. Winning comes by intelligently counteracting the real foes on the field.

We're going to start by identifying the three most formidable enemies of effective communication: the *gaps*, the *noise*, and the *fog*.

Let's begin our journey to clarity in Bordeaux, France—home of great wines and at least one astonishing instance of a very costly communications gap.

The Gaps

> *"It's very important to choose our words very carefully*
> *because miscommunication leads to misunderstanding,*
> *which rarely leads to anything good."*
> **—CHARLES F. GLASSMAN**

THE POINT: Miscommunication is a fact of life.

In 2012, a wealthy Russian oligarch wanted to own property in France, so he bought a historic chateau near the village of Yvrac in Bordeaux.[1]

He contracted with a Polish construction firm to do the renovations, including the removal of a small outbuilding.

Russian owner, Polish workers, French work site—hey, what could go wrong?

A lot, it turns out. The workers mistakenly demolished the entire chateau—razing it to the ground! And, in a final maddening twist, they left the run-down outbuilding standing.

What happened here? Why wasn't everyone on the same page?

- The owner did not make the core intent of the work crystal clear: clean the place up (not destroy it).
- The project leader did not effectively communicate the detailed, specific scope of the project to the workers.
- No one was supervising and course-correcting after the project commenced.

The fault: a gap of some missing (or misunderstood) words. The result: a lot of missing rubles.

There are approximately eight billion people[2] on this planet, speaking about 7,150 different languages. Every individual brings their own life experience, their own perceptions, even their own definitions and meanings to their experience of communication. With all those people, all those languages, and all those differing life experiences, there are infinite ways to fail to communicate.

In our example above, language barriers undoubtedly exacerbated the misunderstandings. At some point in time, we've all struggled to communicate with people from different places speaking different languages.

But language barriers go far beyond the matter of speaking Russian, Polish, or French. We're human, so we're surrounded by many forms of missed communication. Even when we're all supposedly speaking the same tongue, we suffer from other types of language barriers, such as:

- Too much information (TMI) that overwhelms the brain.
- Specialized jargon/acronyms that listeners don't comprehend.
- Vague generalities that leave room for varying interpretations.
- Poorly chosen words that give an unintended meaning.
- Divergent communication styles that don't mesh smoothly.

Simply throwing words out into the void and assuming that an audience will receive and understand them is a surefire recipe for miscommunication. If the connection breaks, the communication short-circuits.

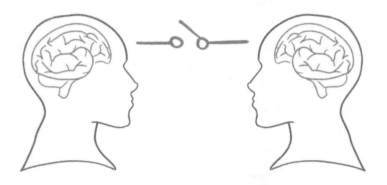

How many times have you walked out of a meeting, confident that everyone had reached a common consensus, only to find out later that every person walked away understanding something different? Happens every day, everywhere.

Turns out that getting people in the same place is much easier than getting people on the same page.

Getting people in the same place is much easier than getting people on the same page.

As we all know, a simple, common phrase like "I love you" carries with it multiple possible meanings. Is it fraternal love? Romantic love? Lustful attraction? How many misunderstandings (and Hollywood movies) has that ambiguous phrase spawned?

We can even catastrophically misunderstand numbers. In 1999, after nearly 10 months of travel to our neighboring red planet, the Mars Climate Orbiter was set to start studying the Martian atmosphere and climate. Instead, this $125-million space probe broke up and burned in the atmosphere. Why?

One set of engineers at the NASA Jet Propulsion Laboratory used the metric system in its calculations, while the builder of the craft, Lockheed Martin, provided critical acceleration data in the imperial system (pounds, feet, inches). This mathematical misalignment was enough to plunge the orbiter to its catastrophic demise.

Do you like big numbers? Here's one striking measure from the world of business. According to the 2022 report[3] by Grammarly and The Harris Poll (*The State of Business Communication*), the annual cost of ineffective communication for US businesses is estimated to be $1.2 trillion. The report highlights some startling numbers:

- Business leaders estimate that their teams lose an average of 7.47 hours per week to poor communication.
- Knowledge workers report spending as much as half of their workweek communicating, with the majority (86 percent) experiencing communication issues during that time.

- The estimated cost of ineffective communications per year for a company of 500 employees is $6,253,000.

Think about that first point. Can you imagine any leader or manager saying, "Hey, it's OK if you spend one day out of five spinning around aimlessly — productivity is optional on Tuesdays." Yet, that's the status quo.

Neither you nor I can afford that sort of drag on efficiency and profitability. Just think about the potential ROI of organizational and team training in effective communications. What if you cut that 20 percent wasted time per week in half across the board?

The impact isn't just corporate, however. Even our mundane efforts to communicate can backfire. Each of us has had to retract or correct something we said to a family member, a neighbor, or a friend. I once lost a month's rent because of a communications gap with a landlord. We didn't put a particular agreement in writing, and ended up with opposing interpretations.

Years ago, my wife commented (regarding hunky male Hollywood/model types) that she "doesn't go for overly handsome men." Of course, it wasn't clear whether her comment was meant to apply to me as well — I've never let her forget that one!

Here's the progression that applying clarity can help us avoid:

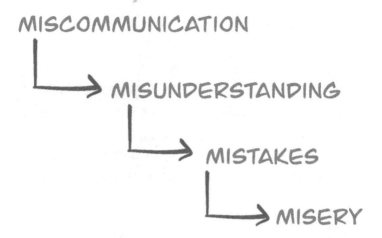

I wish I could offer you a magic wand to wave over your words and make everyone pay attention, find the right meaning, and act accordingly. No such magic implement exists. But here's the next best thing: You can minimize the misunderstanding gaps by designing your communications with the Clarity Fuel Formula.

Which brings us to the next challenge we face: that whole "paying attention" thing I just mentioned. What is stopping people from tuning into you and your message? You might be shocked at the competition you have every day for the brain space of your audience. You and I are up against the fierce and ever-growing Goliath of distraction: noise.

CLARITY SPOTLIGHT

Talk about a high-profile event. The Academy Awards. Live TV. Time for Faye Dunaway and Warren Beatty to open the envelope and announce the 2017 Oscars Best Picture winner.

Beatty was hesitant to say it, so Dunaway pronounced, "And the winner is *La La Land*!" Up came the cast of that movie to give their speeches.

But they weren't the winners. Big mistake.

After a few minutes of embarrassed confusion, the mix-up was corrected. *Moonlight* was actually the winning film. Beatty had been given the envelope for the winner of the category of Lead Actress (which was *La La Land's* Emma Stone).

Not only weren't Dunaway and Beatty on the same page, but the page inside the envelope, supplied by PwC, was incorrect. Even with everyone's advanced preparations, in front all those cameras and lights, someone didn't confirm the delivered message.

Egg never looks good on anyone's face, especially with an audience of millions. Just ask Steve Harvey, after he announced the wrong winner of the Miss Universe contest in 2015.

Noise

Oh, the noise! Oh, the noise! Noise! Noise! Noise! There's one thing I hate! All the NOISE! NOISE! NOISE! NOISE!

—FROM DR. SEUSS'S "HOW THE GRINCH STOLE CHRISTMAS" (1966 CARTOON VERSION ADAPTED BY CHUCK JONES AND BEN WASHAM)

THE POINT: Your biggest competition is not the competition. It's the noise.

It was Christmas Day, 1989, and General Manuel Noriega, repressive military leader of Panama, decided to hole himself up in the Vatican's embassy building after the US military invaded his country. He was hopelessly surrounded but would not give himself up. What's an army to do?

Roll in a fleet of Humvees mounted with loudspeakers and blast the general nonstop with a rock concert for the ages. He got The Clash, U2, Van Halen, The Doors…even Rick Astley (Want the playlist? It's available on YouTube[4]).

By January third, he surrendered. The noise won.

You may not be a dictator-in-hiding, but I guarantee that your attempts to communicate are regularly overwhelmed by the most powerful foe of all—the surrounding noise. We—and our audiences—are inundated 24/7 by an endless tide of audio, video, digital, live, and virtual stimulation.

Businesses always strategize around their biggest competition when trying to gain customer engagement. News flash: that primary competitor is not another company or brand. It's noise.

Trying to win attention? Your biggest hurdle is *everything* that is occupying the mind of your audience. It's a crowded calendar, a ringing phone, a looming deadline, a sick pet. It's Netflix, Twitter, CNN, and Facebook. We even pay dearly to have sophisticated earbuds pour yet more concentrated noise into our ears to drown out all the other ambient noise that surrounds us.

No mute button, no noise cancellation feature, can stop the distractions. Simon & Garfunkel sang about the sound of silence, but you and your audience will rarely experience that luxury.

Have you ever heard the cacophony of reporters yelling out their questions at a White House press conference? It's a wall of sound. Nothing gets through. That's you and me over there in the back row, trying to get somebody to hear us.

Back in 2014, marketing consultant Mark Schaefer coined the phrase "content shock"[5] to describe the overwhelming amount of information available (especially online) that makes it very difficult to be heard. The volume level of the noise is going to keep increasing, with no ceiling in sight. And now we have the looming prospect of being suffocated by AI-generated writing (shall we call that content schlock?). More words from more sources at higher velocity and volume.

Here's what we're up against:

- Worldwide, people spend seven to ten hours per day in front of screens, including 147 minutes per day on social media, with mobile use a growing percentage of that time.[6]
- The average media consumer views 4,000 to 10,000 ads per day[7] (including online ad impressions), and the average professional receives between 75 and 200 emails per day.
- The average number of hourly interruptions for modern workers is ten to twenty.[8]

How many times a day does the average American check their phone? Estimates range from 96 to 350 times per day. Talk about on-demand distraction! That means that every few minutes, we have to *re*-gain attention. Ugh. Nobody ever said this was going to be a fair fight.

All of that noisiness adds up to a lot of competition for the attention of your target audience. In business, we talk a lot about deliverables. Do you realize what your primary "deliverable" is as a communicator? *Focus.* Unless you earn the focus of your audience, nothing else matters.

The people that win in life are focus-earners. Attention-holders. Distraction-beaters.

Think about how you're forced to handle the constant waves of email or other digital messages. With our crowded inbox, it's glance, scan, delete. That's how an HR professional must process piles of resumes or how a prospect digs through a myriad of sales pitches. If something relevant doesn't stand out immediately, it's not a priority.

Even if you're not in the corporate world, your main communication goal is the same: earning focus. No matter the topic, your words and ideas need to rise above the noise and gain attention. Can I get an "Amen!" from every teacher, tour guide, coach, and poet out there?

So, what are the chances of someone noticing and paying attention to your message (let alone remembering and acting on it)? Pretty minimal if you haven't designed it to beat the competition. A clear and compelling signal is the only thing that rises above the noise.

And what is that compelling signal? What does the mind fasten onto? This is huge, so don't miss it—here is your master key to earning focus.

The human brain is seeking immediate, personal relevance—that's the WIIFM (What's In It For Me), which we'll discuss further when we dip into some practical brain science in chapter 2.

The human brain is seeking immediate, personal relevance.

You win when your audience immediately grasps *why* they should be listening. You must couch your message in terms of a felt need, desire, or fear. Machines don't have personal motivations, but people do. They want what they want. People are focused on what matters…to them.

Here's the bad news: Nobody cares about you, your company, or your offering. Ouch. But there's also good news: They might start to care if you succeed in creating a message that speaks to their wants.

The human brain, as a matter of self-preservation, is intensely selfish with its focus. What's in it for me? Is this a priority right now? Is there an important point? If not, into the mental trash can it goes in a matter of seconds. That's the only way to sort through the tsunami of noise.

Social platforms target ads in your feeds about your current interests, needs, and purchases, disturbingly at times. Why? Your posts, your comments, even your lingering attention have tipped off the algorithms about what is relevant to you right now.

If I'm posting about a new winter outfit, advertisers spend their dollars better by showing me clothes (a pre-existing interest) rather than yelling into my feed about grass seed and fertilizer. That would just be noise—until such time as I start posting about lawn care. I have to care before I'm willing to hear.

You must immediately show your audience why they should care about your message because there's too much else in the focus queue fighting for attention. Fight the noise with immediate relevance. First impressions possess outsized importance, which is why you need to get to the point—quickly.

Noise is a tough opponent, but there's yet another enemy out there ready to obscure your message. That's the fog machine.

CLARITY SPOTLIGHT

Shopping for just about anything used to be a pretty confusing and time-consuming process, until Amazon came on the scene, striving to become "Earth's most customer-centric company." Jeff Bezos, the founder, started out with bold clarity of mission.

I don't even want to think about how much money I've spent on that site. The company makes it too easy. Amazon cracked the code on giving customers what they want, the way they want it.

Online immediacy? Check.

Wide selection? Check.

Reviews and recommendations? Check.

Cheap or free shipping? Check.

Intuitive navigation? Check.

Trouble-free returns? Check.

One-click buying? Check.

In other words, Amazon has become the king of WIIFM instant grat-ification, because it tapped into what we want: personal relevance, easy access, and less effort. It's the Easy button (sorry, Staples) of e-commerce.

People want their transactions—including processing informa-tion—to go as effortlessly as possible because that's how the hu-man mind and heart work. You need to spoil people with simplicity, brevity, and ease.

Fog

> "War is the realm of uncertainty; three-quarters of the factors on which action in war is based are wrapped in a fog of greater or lesser uncertainty."
> —CARL VON CLAUSEWITZ

THE POINT: Great communicators clear the fog instead of adding to it.

Decades ago, the US Army War College introduced the acronym VUCA[9] to describe what has often been called "the fog of war." Before any planned military engagement, there are usually clear goals, strategies, and tactics. Then the first bullets fly, and all hell breaks loose.

The combatants are now surrounded by the confusing fog of war. Nobody knows what is coming next. The best illustration of this reality is the D-Day landing depicted in the first half-hour of the film *Saving Private Ryan*. Months of meticulous battle planning devolved into instant chaos once the soldiers came into contact with the enemy.

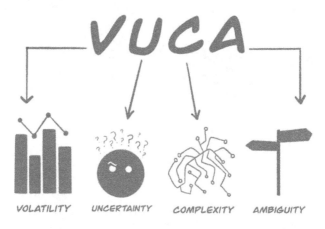

VOLATILITY   UNCERTAINTY   COMPLEXITY   AMBIGUITY

Business and life are often like a chaotic battlefield. Business leaders have adopted the Army's VUCA acronym to portray the reality of the environment we all live in every day.

The COVID-19 pandemic showed us how a crippling dose of VUCA is never more than a moment away. The world has always been volatile, but during those years of confusion, we saw how individuals and groups suffered tremendously when everything—economics, healthcare, social and civil order—was shrouded in ambiguity.

I never did get sick with the virus, but my life was thoroughly disrupted, nonetheless. My business nearly went under. My clients struggled with paralysis and doubt. And the school where my wife teaches was constantly trying to juggle and improvise. The daily weight of uncertainty was immensely discouraging for everyone.

For many weary months, there was no clarity, only questions without answers. Fog is charming at the Golden Gate Bridge, but it's the last thing a VUCA-afflicted listener needs. We humans don't thrive well in a VUCA state. People need stability. A sense of direction. Predictability. Answers.

Fog clouds the mind. To be productive, healthy, and hopeful, people at every age and stage of life need clarity instead of confusion. That's true on the big stage of something like a global pandemic, but it's just as true in the workplace when an employee needs to know what is expected of them day to day.

Stephen Covey summed it up well: "If there's one thing that's certain in business, it's uncertainty."

Foggy communication is everywhere. Fuzzy marketing messages. Imprecise directions. Cryptic emails. You don't want to add to the confusion with ambiguous words and half-formed notions.

One of the biggest enemies here is the overuse of jargon. So many emails, websites, and presentations are loaded with important-sounding terms that, put together, add up to meaningless bluster. Like this generic fogbank: "Welcome to _____! Our Mission is to be the most trusted provider of innovative solutions that empower all stakeholders across the healthcare continuum to deliver world-class outcomes."

Can't picture what this company actually does? Neither can I. That's because they just fogged our glasses with a steaming stew of vague nonsense.

Many efforts at professional communication resemble gibberish, unstructured information dumps that waste the time of the audience. According to Josh Bernoff, author of the book *Writing Without Bullsh*t*, this careless approach is not only inefficient, it is also disrespectful to the people who have to expend energy finding the point.[10] It's not enough to convey words; you must highlight the most important idea or ideas and structure the writing so that people can quickly grasp the flow of thought.

Bernoff talks about his Iron Imperative for writers: "treat the reader's time as more valuable than your own." Practicing clarity means that you do the work, so your listeners don't have to.

> **Practicing clarity means that you do the work, so your listeners don't have to.**

I have seen a multitude of job postings that include fifteen or twenty bullet points of responsibilities for the candidate. They often contain generic and ambiguous nonsense like this:

1. Interact with all relevant stakeholders to establish best practices.
2. Consult with new and existing customers to develop success plans that drive value.
3. Discover additional opportunities to enhance existing lines of business.
4. Communicate regularly with supervisors and direct reports.
5. Align with Sales, Marketing, and Compliance to document success-forward synergies.
6. KPIs. Do all the KPIs. Whatever they might be.

Boilerplate, non-prioritized, foggy job descriptions are a form of professional malpractice. People need clear specifics, not vague generalities. Ambiguity is definitely not a communication best practice.

The opposite of clarification—what I call "foggification"—is a sure way to set people up for failure. Ann Latham opens her book *The Power of Clarity* with the story[11] of a VP giving the directive, "Look into this," to a new marketing employee. She and her team spent three weeks researching the issue and presented a comprehensive report. But the eye-rolling VP apparently only wanted a gut reaction summary that would have taken ten minutes. A simple clarification would have saved a lot of face for everyone involved.

(I sometimes wear a T-shirt, designed in the style of a lighted Las Vegas sign, that states, *AMBIGUITY: What Happens in Vagueness, Stays in Vagueness*. It does earn me some side-eyes and smirks at the gym.)

"To be unclear is to be unkind," is a phrase often quoted by financial guru Dave Ramsey. Handing out more VUCA is not doing anyone any favors. Stability, certainty, simplicity, and directness should be what we strive for with our words. Clear the fog to activate and energize people.

So, how do you clear the fog, rise above the noise, and bridge the gaps? By designing all your communications with your audience in mind. Here's where the math turns in your favor. There may be 8 billion different people on the planet, but, amazingly, our brains have a common set of criteria for receiving messages. We're all different, but we have a common mental operating system.

Every one of those billions of brains have the same cardinal, unspoken, inflexible mandate: *Give me the information I want the way I want it*. Every human has this unspoken request: *Make it easy*. As you're about to discover, knowing how to craft words in a brain-friendly way (for easy processing) is key to effective communication design that overcomes all the barriers.

CLARITY SPOTLIGHT

I hate jargon. You probably do, too. We're not alone.

That's why there's a book devoted to it: Why Business People Speak Like Idiots: A Bullfighter's Guide.[12] I wish I'd written this book. So much fun.

From the inner flap (tongue in cheek):

"This is just the kind of synergistic, customer-centric, upsell-driven, out-of-the-box, customizable, strategically tactical, best-of-breed thought leadership that will help our clients track to true north."

You've been there, haven't you? Maybe you've even uttered such claptrap.

The opening of the book tells it like it is: "Let's face it: Business today is drowning in bullsh*t...bull has become the language of business. This is troubling, because almost any time we need to deliver a message at work, it's because we need to persuade someone to think or do something...you have a huge opportunity to become more persuasive. To be that one infectious human voice—the one that's authentic and original and makes people want to listen."

The best way to combat jargon is to simply shine a light on how shallow and unilluminating it really is. That's why you'll regularly find egregious examples of jargoneering highlighted in my LinkedIn feed.

CHAPTER 2:

The Brain

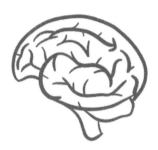

Getting your message across to others is daunting. You're up against the confusion and distractions of an oversaturated world. You're one voice in a maelstrom of sensory stimulation.

And, to add to the hardship, your primary customer (the human brain) is selfish and impatient. Every brain has a permanent case of the Terrible Twos—gimme what I want, right now! I want it my way!

Instead of thinking of this demand as a problem, however, consider it as your strategic advantage. Because once you know the rules about how the brain works, you can design your communication so that you are one of the few who gets through. You just need to know what signals the brain is tuned to and package your information accordingly.

You're about to learn some things about yourself—specifically, how your brain does its job—that perhaps you never knew. And as a communicator, these bits of practical brain science are about to become your best assets—and your strategic allies.

Meet the Gatekeeper

"The average attention span of the modern human being is about half as long as whatever you're trying to tell them."
—MEG ROSOFF

THE POINT: The brain's master filter attends to what is most relevant, so you need to get to the point right away.

The human brain is a very busy place. In fact, your brain is processing about eleven million bits of information[13] every second from all five senses. Not only is that a colossal number, but it also naturally leads to the following question: How do we process that torrent of sensory data and not become utterly insane ourselves in the process? What decides which pieces of information matter most?

The answer is magic; well, maybe about as close to magic as we can imagine. Processing and sorting all that nervous system data is the job of a brain structure called the reticular activating system, or RAS.[14] This neurobiological marvel attached to our brain stem is responsible for filtering input, regulating our sleep/wake cycles, and activating our fight-or-flight response.

The RAS is the gatekeeper of focus. It is the supervisor of our attention span. As a communicator, it is your worst enemy and your best friend (if you know the cheat codes).

As we go about our day, we're not even aware of all the work that the RAS is doing. What we *are* aware of at any moment is whatever the RAS has elevated to our conscious notice, while it pushes everything else into the background as noise. It is the bouncer at the front door of our consciousness, and it only allows the VIPs (Very Important Priorities) through.

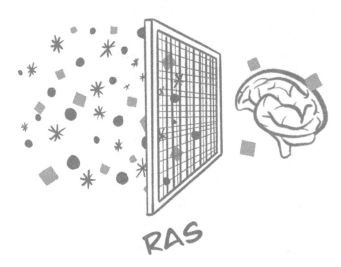

RAS

Who or what are those VIPs? Here's the secret: The RAS pays attention to things that are new, surprising, interesting, threatening, or specific. It elevates what is different or changing and pushes aside the same-old-same-old. The RAS is on the lookout for information of immediate, personal importance, and it is always making split-second decisions about what truly matters right now.

In other words, the VIP is immediate personal relevance.

A continual refrain for salespeople is that they need to quickly get to the customer's personal desire—their WIIFM—if they want to gain a hearing. As it turns out, that's actually true of all forms of communication. The RAS is always tuned to one radio station: WIIFM. Relevance is the signal. Everything else is static.

If your RAS decided to go on strike, you'd become a quivering mass of stupefied Jell-O on the floor, unable to distinguish the importance of one thing from another.

You and I are hardwired to be selfishly selective. It's a survival mechanism. Your brain will attend to messages that pique your interest and speak to your priorities. As a communicator, you can take full advantage of this fundamental law of brain function by appealing right away to personal desire.

So, aim your communications arrows directly at the target: the RAS. That's the front door—the only way in.

You don't have hours or even minutes to secure attention, you have seconds. That's not my rule. That's a brain rule.

> **You don't have hours or even minutes to secure attention, you have seconds.**

That is why we experience such frustration when a someone meanders around and doesn't make clear what the purpose or the benefit of their communication is. How you package your message in the first moments determines whether you gain a hearing or just become part of the background noise.

You need to front-load your class, sermon, book, presentation, meeting, website, article, email, conference call, or networking introduction with something strikingly interesting. In a sense, you're always selling, and the person you're addressing wants to know why they should listen.

Here's an example of a terrible opening paragraph, with no VIP in sight:

"As a dynamic and results-driven consultancy we offer a range of cutting-edge solutions designed to optimize your business operations and enhance your organizational performance. Leveraging our deep expertise in various business domains and our proficiency in advanced analytical tools and techniques, we specialize in delivering strategic insights and actionable recommendations that drive sustainable growth and value creation."

This blather might be effective for putting someone to sleep, but it doesn't tap into relevance and desire, and it's obviously RAS-hostile. Countless websites and sales pitches start with such snoozer language. That's not aiming at the target, it's shooting yourself in the foot!

How about this approach instead: "Our clients average a 22 percent increase in profitability when we transform their underutilized CRM platform into a powerhouse of fresh leads." Striking, specific, relevant—I want increased profitability, I want optimal resource utilization, and I want fresh leads. Tell me more!

Smart targeting is what leads to "Tell me more!" A new Australian coffee shop opening up in Franklin, Tennessee? I'm all ears. That's got a WIIFM. (Actually, a lot of this book was written in that shop—Elroy Coffee Co.)

An expanded koala veterinary clinic across the globe in Sydney? A dust storm in Melbourne? Not ringing my bell of relevance. But for someone living in Australia, those items are far more relevant than some coffee shop in Franklin.

(Did you know that Australia is wider than the moon? I didn't. More on that later.)

Let's consider the numbers. If you and I are sitting down at Elroy for a discussion, maybe with a couple of the shop's delicious sausage rolls, that person-to-person interaction takes up about 60 bits per second[15] of sensory information. Everything else is noise. We must somehow find ways to rise above 10,999,940 million bits of internal and external competition to get into the winner's circle of conscious focus. A daunting challenge.

Author Milo O. Frank, in the book How to Get Your Point Across in 30 Seconds or Less, explains: "Your deals, jobs, money, and success can all hang on first impressions. Isn't it true that with just a few words, an image is formed in your mind and in theirs, and you and they act accordingly? Often, there's only time for a few words, so they better be the right ones...to survive and move ahead in business or in any other relationship, you must be able to get your point across swiftly and succinctly, in 30 seconds or less."[16]

So, how do you make your words a clear signal amid all the surrounding stimuli? How do you gain that precious asset of focus? I'll get to that formula in the upcoming chapters (Hint: It has a lot to do with the power of shortcuts).

Let's think about this positively. Since you know that the RAS is the gatekeeper of information, you know that a clear WIIFM is your VIP pass through the door. That presents a huge opportunity for you as a communication designer. When you know how to be RAS-friendly, you have a strategic advantage over all the others who are clamoring for attention. You can learn how to design your communications to win the focus battle.

Match the Meaning

> *"An order that can be misunderstood, will be misunderstood."*
> **—NAPOLEON BONAPARTE**

THE POINT: Explaining, not assuming, is what allows us to arrive at shared meaning.

"Pick up some tomatoes for me."

You say to-may-toe, I say to-mah-toe. The slight difference in pronunciation is pretty harmless, but what if I actually think a tomato is a coconut? If you send me to the grocery store, tonight's spaghetti sauce may end up with a sunscreen-like tropical flavor.

Not too many people will confuse a tomato for a coconut, but as I described earlier, there is always plenty of room for misunderstandings. In fact, there are many different kinds of tomatoes. If I think "some tomatoes" equals four beefsteaks, and you actually wanted twelve Roma tomatoes, then our assumptions are out of sync.

That's what I call the "mental metadata" problem. Metadata is *information about information*—descriptive tags, if you will. We are constantly, if unconsciously, storing ideas and memories with associated words, feelings, and experiences. A unique word cloud of metadata surrounds our memories. We each carry around our own hidden assumptions and definitions.

Our brains are metadata machines, jam-packed with a variety of words and meanings.

Vizzini: *"Inconceivable!"*
Inigo Montoya: *"You keep using that word. I do not
think it means what you think it means."*
—THE PRINCESS BRIDE MOVIE

Social media apps like Twitter and Instagram use the term (and symbol) "hashtags" to signal metadata. When you #hashtag a picture or a post, those descriptive labels add context that surrounds the message with additional elements of meaning.

An element of communications clarity is getting our unspoken hashtags synchronized.

Aligned expectations require careful explanations. Voltaire put it this way: "If you wish to converse with me, define your terms."

"If you wish to converse with me, define your terms."

Why does a skillful server in a restaurant ask you a series of clarifying questions when you place your meal order? Simple—they want to make sure they convey your desires accurately to the kitchen. Everybody looks and feels bad when a food order is blown.

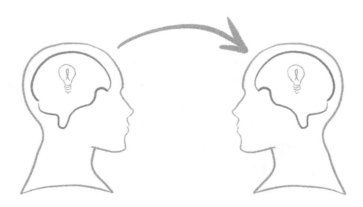

A pharmaceutical client I knew once contracted with an agency for a document called a "backgrounder." The agency spent a lot of time and money and delivered something that was far too long and complex for the purpose, which was to provide a brief, straightforward explanation. Each party had assumed their own meaning for "backgrounder" and took a common understanding for granted. This mismatched metadata problem is one of the biggest issues in effective project management.

How can you overcome the challenge of mismatched meaning? Here's one approach I use all the time: When I'm concerned that my audience may not have a common understanding, I'll use a word or phrase and then I'll say, *and what I mean by that is...* and add a clarifying definition, example, or illustration.

This is particularly important when using technical terms. A software programmer might use the words "intuitive UI design," but a listener could easily misunderstand that phrase without an explanation such as, "what that means is user interface design—creating ways that people interact with a program so that it is simple to access, understand, and use."

One of the great challenges for any consultant is to get into the head of the client and get their meaning out in a clear fashion. Copywriting expert Thomas Clifford uses a technique he calls inSync Copywriting to efficiently arrive at matched meaning. Instead of wasting time, money, and resources emailing documents back and forth, he cowrites in real time with B2B (business-to-business) consulting clients in Google Docs. This means he's exactly in sync with his clients' thinking and capturing their expertise with 100 percent accuracy.

One of my favorite sayings (often attributed to George Bernard Shaw though the actual origin is disputed), is: "The single biggest problem in communication is the illusion that it has taken place." Whenever I highlight that phrase, everyone in the audience reacts knowingly. We've all been there.

(As an aside, I can also assure you, from personal experience, that having your book rigorously edited by a pair of expert eyes is an exercise in having your unspoken assumptions and inaccurate meanings brought to the surface—and paying dearly for the privilege! Thanks, Josh.)

Unspoken mental metadata is a fact of life. Assuming that words automatically convey accurate meaning is an illusion you need to dispense with posthaste. Never assume a synced understanding. Always be ready to explain, define, and clarify. That's part of being a brain-friendly illuminator.

And since that brain is also processing a huge amount of other information at any given time, you've got to make the meaning clear quickly.

Know the Limits

> *"Simple and to the point is always the best way to get your point across."*
> —GUY KAWASAKI

THE POINT: It's your job to skillfully plant the right ideas in the limited brain space you're allocated.

As I've shown, "crazy busy" doesn't even begin to describe what's going on inside each of our skulls. In fact, while your brain represents about 2 percent of your total body weight, it uses roughly 20 percent of your energy[17] every day.

That leads to this question: How many unallocated resources are there in any audience's mind for what you and I have to say?

Answer: very few.

I like to put it this way: Unless you're a close relative or friend, you've got about one pixel of space in my mind. That's a small piece of memory real estate. Sure, it's a mixed metaphor, but it makes the point, right?

When Amazon needs to store more information, it just builds a new data center. Our brains don't have that luxury. We don't get to spawn new brain centers to increase our capacity to process and remember stuff.

We live in an interconnected world of exploding information density where a million things are clamoring for our attention all the time.

As much as we'd like to believe that we, and our messages, are the most important thing in everyone's world, the fact is, what we have to say is just one of a vast number of things someone must process that day. If the audience-brain has to work too hard to figure us out, it just…won't.

Why do we instinctively put off reading a long, complicated email? Because our brain intuitively senses that "this is too much work!" Our instinct is to avoid more effort: more thinking, more processing, more to remember, more to do. Who wants that?

When explaining your business, your lesson, or your message, you feel pressure to include more, not less. Big mistake. That's just overwhelming the brain and making it less likely that the right message will get through the RAS and gain its memory pixel. This is why you must condense your message to the smallest size possible. The goal is compressed, not comprehensive. When it comes to getting a message across, less is more.

When it comes to getting a message across, less is more.

Nowhere is this truer than in professional networking. You have only a sliver of time to make a good impression.

In fact, when introducing yourself, you should reduce the classic "elevator pitch" to something more like a sound bite: what I call a "memory dart." (I have an entire chapter on crafting memory darts in my book *Clarity Wins.*)

Lawyers, bankers, wealth advisors, realtors—these people all face the challenge of standing out among so many others with the same title. But there's one lawyer, J.K., I always remember because of the memory dart she uses to introduce herself: "I went to law school, so you don't have to." She doesn't give a boring, long-winded explanation of the landscape of law practice. She just uses an amusing and memorable phrase.

You're transmitting into an environment of gaps, noise, and fog. You're addressing a brain with a rigorous gatekeeper, a bunch of assorted metadata, and not much capacity for extra work. Your words will either work for you or against you. "Brevity in writing is the best insurance for its perusal," says Rudolf Virchow.

CLARITY SPOTLIGHT

Brain science is endlessly fascinating. There is so much that we don't yet know, and scientists are advancing and refining theories continuously.

New York Times best-selling author Daniel J. Levitin goes deep in his book *The Organized Mind*[18] to explain how the human brain processes its way through the whirlwind of information. He calls one of those concepts "decision overload."

"In 1976, the average supermarket stocked 9,000 unique products; today that number has ballooned to 40,000 of them, yet the average person gets 80-85% of their needs in only 150 different supermarket items. That means we have to ignore 39,850 items in the store...All this ignoring and deciding comes with a cost. Neuroscientists have discovered that unproductivity and loss of drive can result from decision overload."

Extrapolate this to every other area of life, because the growing volume of information and the need to sort, evaluate, and decide is not declining—it's going up. On all fronts. Think about how hard it's become just to decide which streaming movie to watch on any given night!

In light of all that I've covered so far, let's summarize: What does brain-*hostile* communication design look like? Here are four worst-practice prohibitions:

You Shall Not Overwhelm

That audience—one person or many—has a brain that is already inundated with sensory input. You are not to overload their neurons by dumping too much information, too rapidly, in an unfocused way. Is it not disrespectful of others' time and energy to make their day harder?

The Hippocratic Oath for doctors is simple: First, do no harm. Your number one axiom as a great communicator is similar: First, do not overwhelm. Not in a presentation. Not on a website home page. Not in an email.

Overwhelm = shut down. Your audience needs a drink, not a waterboarding session. Deliver a meal, not a smorgasbord.

Instead of draining the energy of others, you must do the design work yourself, making your message accessible and easy to process.

You Shall Not Confuse

Vague statements, run-on sentences, technical jargon, unstructured information—all of these add to the fog and noise. If your message recipient must do the work of interpreter, that leaves all kinds of room for misunderstanding.

You've heard the expression, "clear as mud"? Not a reputation you want to earn.

Confusion = paralysis and mistakes. Don't contribute to the plague of vague. Except for philosophers, people are looking for answers, not more questions.

Instead of sowing more uncertainty, you can practice simplicity, being as plain and as specific as possible so that there is minimal chance of setting others up for failure.

You Shall Not Waste Time

Time is a precious and nonrenewable resource. The business world demands systems that are streamlined, focused, and efficient. That includes our communications. Every back-and-forth, every error, every missed signal is a misallocation of resources.

Time is money. Don't waste both.

Squandered time = squandered opportunity. Brevity wins. Get right to the point.

The amount of time the RAS allocates to secure attention and engagement is ridiculously small, which means that you need to pack as much meaning into as few words as possible.

You Shall Not Assume

If you can be misunderstood, you will be misunderstood. That's the human experience. When you realize that people have different backgrounds, experiences, and mental metadata, you develop the instinct to be more careful to explain your meaning. Even if words are understood, intentions and expectations may not be.

Assumptions can lead to talking past one another. So, explain, align, and document. If you're going to err, err on the side of clarifying.

Always summarize, in simple terms, and in writing, so that people do not walk away with undetected misunderstandings.

We can wrap up all four of these cardinal sins into one master prohibition: *You Shall Not Obfuscate.* To obfuscate is to render unclear, obscure, or unintelligible. My first book was titled *Clarity Wins.* It could easily have had the subtitle, *Obfuscation Loses.*

Obfuscation freezes up the mental and emotional operating system. Instead, we can each become accomplished wordsmiths (definition: one who uses words skillfully). We can be copywriters fueled by human (not artificial) intelligence.

Jack Appleman, who teaches successful business writing principles in corporate and academic settings, says that the biggest problem he consistently encounters with his coaching clients (many with extensive technical expertise)

is that they don't know how to start with a simple explanation of the big picture.[19] They revert to a default setting in their mental operating system of giving too much
background and detail, both in writing and speaking. Jack
helps these executives develop a simple opening statement
(BLUF, or bottom line up front) and then provide fast
context: a quick summary that frames the rest of the material in a focused way.

So, the human brain knows what it doesn't want.
What it does want is clarity. Before we finish this section,
let's take a moment to define more carefully what we mean
by the word "clarity."

Here's my working definition of clarity: *focused ideas
expressed in brain-friendly words.* In this book, I'll outline
dozens of ways to craft the most effective words you can
use to light up your listeners' brains. But beneath each
clearly expressed message is focus: a specific idea, purpose,
goal, or intent. Focused clarity of thought fuels clarity of
expression.

I see the necessity for focused clarity in at least four
dimensions:

1. Clarity of purpose (Purpose: answers the Why?)
2. Clarity of direction (Strategic direction: answers
   the Where?)
3. Clarity of expectations (Leading others: answers
   the What and How?)
4. Clarity of expression (How can we get our message
   across to others effectively?)

Clarity: Focused ideas expressed in brain-friendly words.

Much of this book will focus on #4 – clarity of expression – but you'll easily notice how the other dimensions of focused clarity feed into our effective use of words.

I once attempted to let my wife know about something while I was away doing a client workshop (ironically, on the topic of communications clarity). I didn't have much time, so I did her the "favor" of sending unclear, piecemeal messages that left her utterly bewildered. I admitted to her that I had violated all my communication principles. Chagrined, I also told the client team what I did as an example of what to avoid. We've all done it, right?

Which brings me to my radically obvious thesis: Every single human being on this planet can benefit from applying the practical methods of gaining, and communicating with, clarity. No exceptions. CEOs and salespeople. Parents and pastors. IT professionals and marketers. Authors and social media influencers. Every company, every job title, every function—at any age and in any language. Clarity of ideas and words applies everywhere.

I have spent the majority of my career in the world of business (specifically, in healthcare and life sciences), as you'll readily notice from many of the examples I will cite. My career roles have always centered on the skillful use of words. Sales. Training. Marketing. Writing. Consulting. Confession: I've had countless words fall flat and not produce their intended result. It's relatively easy to make machines exchange information accurately with one another. Humans? Not so much.

However, the framework I'm outlining actually applies to everyone, in any realm of human endeavor. If you interact with humans and use words, you need to practice clarity.

> **If you interact with humans and use words, you need to practice clarity.**

The need for clarity is not a new idea. Philosophers, linguists, writers, and speakers have underscored the need to use words skillfully for millennia. A well-known saying commonly attributed to Hippocrates sums it up well: "The chief virtue that language can have is clearness."

Words have a noble purpose—to illuminate; to clear the fog and turn the lights on. You may not be a member of the Illuminati, but I hope you will join the ranks of highly skilled illuminators.

So, starting right now, I am bestowing upon you a new title: *communication designer.* (Actually, you already have this title; I'm just making you aware of it). My goal with this book is to make sure you are *highly effective* at designing your communications by practicing brevity, simplicity, and clarity in your word use, whatever your role in business or in life. (Unless you're a zombie. Then your intentions are quite clear with grunts alone.)

- Want to succeed at leadership? You need to become a skilled communication designer.

- Want to sell or market effectively? You need to become a skilled communication designer.
- Want to have a powerful brand purpose and message? You need to become a skilled communication designer.
- Want to make an impact with presentations, lessons, and sermons? You need to become a skilled communication designer.
- Want to advance in your career? You need to become a skilled communication designer.
- Want people to read and act on your emails? You need to become a skilled communication designer.

And in a world where artificial intelligence is making deep inroads in the production of words, it is even more imperative that we humans become more skillful, more creative, and more able to connect with fellow humans through clear communications craftsmanship.

You can do this. You can rise above the noise. You can turn the lights on in the minds of others. In this book, you will learn the straightforward *rules* of clear communication, and you will acquire the practical *tools* to achieve it.

CLARITY SPOTLIGHT

Professional copywriters are (or should be) some of the best at crafting words that work, avoiding jargon, vagueness, and other sins—the way a script writer and film producer would.

In 2009, Thomas Clifford[20] quit being a documentary filmmaker after 23 award-winning years, thanks to the financial crash. After producing and directing 650 marketing films, he knew storytelling; but he had no other skills (or so he thought), so he was in a deep, scary black hole.

But I knew Tom was a great interviewer. He understood what clear messaging and conversational content looked like. How about applying the same skills to written content? His identity didn't need to change; it was just a matter of gaining clarity about the right medium. He fell in love with copywriting, because it was marketing, sales, and storytelling all rolled into one. Just without film.

Tom soon discovered that there was an abundance of jargony writing in the B2B world, with tons of vagueness and very little clarity. The cardinal sins of communication were splattered everywhere. He asked himself: Who was writing this stuff? His answer: I should be...but without all that jargon! And thus began the next stage in his creative journey.

Part 2:

The Clarity Fuel Formula Rules

Succeeding as a communication designer is a lot like following a recipe. You assemble the correct ingredients and put them together in a sequential process to create a tasty result.

The result, in this case, is becoming brain-friendly with our words.

The Clarity Fuel Formula Rules consist of a four-step process you can follow for all forms of communication.

(Please note that this framework is primarily intended for *planned, purposeful communications using words.* The Clarity Fuel Formula is not about body language and facial expressions; nor is it intended for informal dialogue, sports team cheers, pillow talk, and party conversations.)

It's comforting to realize that are knowable rules for effective human communication. Our brains are designed to take in information from our senses, recognize the familiar, analyze the new, assign meaning, and draw conclusions.

I've already mentioned the highest-level rule: The brain wants what it wants the way it wants it. Our job is to conform our communication to those specific brain-wants. As I noted earlier, the human brain has an operating system. Operating systems run on rules. When you cooperate with the operating system, you win.

Origami is a folding process. Clear communication is an unfolding process. Any speaker can dump a bunch of unstructured, crumpled up information on an audience. For people to absorb our message properly, however, you need to serve it up skillfully.

I once worked as a waiter in a four-star French restaurant. The dining experience would be ruined if I brought out dessert first, dropped the check, piled up the salad with the main course, and finished with an appetizer. That's breaking the rules.

Effective communication does not happen by chance. We're going to examine four logical, brain-friendly steps you can apply to minimize obfuscation and randomness and maximize effective communication:

1. **You Shall Have a Point (Strategize).** Before you begin to compose words, determine the exact purpose and intention of the communication. Why this email, meeting, presentation, or book chapter? What's the anticipated outcome?

2. **You Shall Get to the Point (Sequence).** Frontload your message with something striking and relevant that will instantly capture attention.

3. **You Shall Get the Point Across (Simplify).** Design your message with definitions, illustrations, and shortcuts that will overcome any mental metadata differences, light up the brain, and create meaning and memory.

4. **You Shall Get on the Same Page (Solidify).** Document conclusions, create clear summaries, and outline specific calls to action that everyone can

sign off on. This is especially important for any kind of collaborative effort.

Every part of this formula is something you can apply immediately, but you won't outgrow these practices, because communicating effectively is a lifelong endeavor. You're going to become a top chef of communication!

CHAPTER 3:

You Shall Have a Point

"People with goals succeed because
they know where they're going."
—EARL NIGHTINGALE

As I've listened to someone droning on and on, I've said this dozens of times: "Okay, but what's your point?" It's not my job to figure out your point by sifting through a mass of verbiage. You may be burying the point...or, worse, you may not even *have* one.

What is "the point"? In my definition, the point is your purpose and your intended result distilled to a simple phrase you can share with others. "Begin with the end in mind," famously advised author Stephen Covey.

Simply put: *Strategize* before you speak.

If you're presenting, you're doing so with an intention. You intend to inform people about certain information.

Maybe you're teaching or training on a subject, seeking to smooth out a tense situation, or looking to sell a specific service. By whatever method you're communicating, you want your audience (whether one person or many) to walk away with x as a result.

When President John F. Kennedy was rallying the nation to compete with the USSR in the space race, he articulated a very clear point: land a man on the moon before the end of the 1960s. "We choose to go to the moon in this decade" was his simple declaration. There was no doubt about the intended goal.

You must define that point for yourself before you can get it across to others. Otherwise, it's like expecting a GPS to "just get me there" without bothering to plug in a destination.

When you articulate the point, you answer the unspoken questions "Why?" and "Where are we going?"

> **When you articulate the point, you answer the unspoken questions "Why?" and "Where are we going?"**

Here's a fun exercise. Look in your email Sent folder, review five of your most recent messages, and see if you can create a one-sentence summary of the main point of each message (your purpose or intended result). Then do the same with five emails that others have sent to your inbox.

You'll probably find some head-scratchers. If the recipient can't identify the main point, it's unlikely the email is going to be effective.

To fix this, you can spell out, in advance, the desired objective of every communication—the point. Think about it with this simple model: the A-to-B Shift.

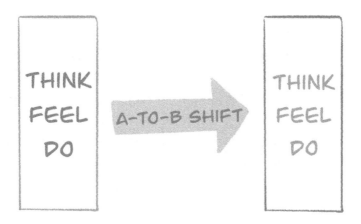

Here's how it works:
- The audience (one or many) is thinking, feeling, and acting a certain way right now. That's the status quo: Point A.
- How do you want your audience to think, feel, and act differently based on your communication? What is the desired specific change? That's Point B.

That shift from A to B *is* the point. That's the purpose, the intended outcome. You must first paint the picture for yourself so you can then sketch it out for others.

Let's consider a common business example. A sales manager may be coaching one of her field sales reps who is failing at pre-call planning. The sales rep has a wing-it mentality because they have a strong gift of gab.

The sales rep employs a defective process and needs a specific remedy.

"You are talking too much and planning too little" may be a true critique, but it is not a clearly articulated, actionable point. Much better: "Skipping pre-call planning is making your customer interaction less effective. You need to spend fifteen minutes before each call reviewing recent contacts with this customer and developing a targeted message about the expanded applications we now address, especially emphasizing these two success stories." That's a well-thought-out point, including a tangible shift in activities.

Only targeted and practical coaching can lead to measurable results.

And when it comes to leading teams, it's very important not to neglect the feelings part of the formula. Like many other parents, I have watched my kids participate in many levels of sports. The best coaches are the ones that detect how the various children are feeling about their performance and then project a can-do confidence to their young charges. They want the kids to feel charged-up about taking on the challenges ahead, not fearful and deflated.

An organizational leader may notice that the viewpoints of the company seem stale and fossilized. She might come to a leadership meeting and say, "we need more diversity here." That may be true, but it's too vague to be actionable. Far better to say, "During the next 18 months, we need to hire or promote at least three senior managers in their 30s who have a leading-edge understanding of technology and the youth market. How can we best accomplish this?"

Having a point and articulating it plainly is a way of setting others up for success. If they know specifically what is intended, it's far easier for them to react appropriately. Vagueness leaves everyone frustrated.

Why does a DoubleTree Hotel hand you a warm chocolate chip cookie at check-in? The company wants you to feel welcome and happy. And it wants you to remember that feeling and choose it again the next time you travel. And tell others about your experience, which I just did.

When I sit down with individuals and businesses to map out their strategic direction and message, what is my highest-level purpose? Simple: I want them to think accurately about how their skills and drives can match up to specific opportunities, feel hopeful and confident about their future, and be able to tell others in the clearest possible terms what they are looking to accomplish.

That's the destination on my clarity GPS.

People need to know the why, and they need to envision the goal. If you want to move others, you need to make sure they—and you—know what the point is.

CLARITY SPOTLIGHT

Airlines are big, complicated organizations that often seem faceless. Maybe even interchangeable—I mean, planes are planes, right? When Herb Kelleher cofounded Southwest Airlines, however, he marched to a different drumbeat.[21] He wanted the flying experience to be enjoyable. He wanted his people to spread the love (in fact, to this day, the company's stock symbol is LUV).

Business gurus used to apply the business school conundrum to him: Who comes first? Your shareholders, your employees, or your customers? Kelleher responded that employees come first, and if employees are treated right, they treat the outside world right, the outside world uses the company's product again, and that makes the shareholders happy.

Kelleher knew that if his employees had a great work experience, they would provide a great flying experience. So he strove for organizational clarity—a fun, caring, human-centric atmosphere that would make air travel a pleasure—as the precursor, and means, to profitability.

Like all airlines, Southwest has had its share of challenges and missteps, but it built the DNA of the organization on a shift in how people can (and should) feel about flying.

CHAPTER 4:

You Shall Get to the Point

"There are four basic premises of writing: clarity, brevity, simplicity, and humanity."

—WILLIAM ZINSSER

Whether you're designing a book, a presentation, a meeting, or an email, the most important thing you can do is to quickly let your audience know why they should tune in.

Keeping your audience in suspense while you wander in the wilderness is not being a good information tour guide. Some people spend so much time trying to get to the point that they simply...don't. At least, not while anyone is still listening.

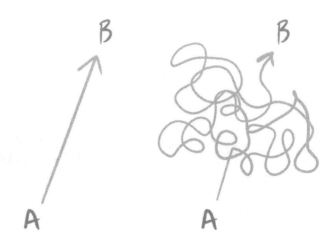

Don't make us wait. I hate waiting. If I want to meander around to Point B, I'll just watch the extended movie edition of *The Return of the King*, with its seven piled-up endings.

How do you get to the point without being abrupt or contrived? It's quite simple. Perhaps after a brief, polite introduction, you deliver a front-loaded value statement. The email that gets a look has a hook. The website that gets right to a relevant point creates engagement.

In other words: design an effective *sequence*.

The human brain needs a sensible flow—a smart arrangement—to be engaged. For example, here is one design sequence that I use regularly:

1. **A**ttention—Take the first few moments to grab those 60 bits of focus.
2. **R**elevance—Immediately let the RAS know why this interaction matters.

3. **I**nformation—Now you've earned the right to share more details.
4. **A**ction—You should share this, if the communication has an anticipated result or call to action, once engagement is already taking place.

GAIN ATTENTION
SHOW RELEVANCE
SHARE INFORMATION
CALL TO ACTION

Thirty-second TV ads for medications use this pattern very effectively. Why? Because it's intuitive. It's orderly. It's brain-friendly. Here's the medical problem. Here's the solution. Here are some facts you need to know, including side effects. Action: Talk to your doctor about x.

Effective website marketers seek to grab attention, lead prospects deeper into information, and then secure action. So do great preachers, motivational speakers, and sales-people. So can you.

What are some of the first lessons kids learn with toys, words, and letters? Putting things in the proper order.

Say you're selling Girl Scout cookies door-to-door. First, you ring the doorbell. Then you introduce yourself and state your purpose. You then give a quick sketch of the message you're seeking to impart and, perhaps, issue a call to action ("Please buy twelve boxes!").

You don't break into my house, take my money, then ring the doorbell on the way out. By sequencing, we recognize that the human psyche is most comfortable with sensible first-this-then-that patterns.

Effective sermon design uses just such a sequence. Start with an attention-grabbing opening. Briefly sketch out the practical relevance and overall importance. Do a deeper dive into exposition of the text. Close with specific applications.

Even the classic marriage proposal uses a sequence like this, starting with the attention-grabbing kneel-and-ring-reveal, to the profession of love and intention, to the closing call to action ("Will you marry me?"). (Just don't screw it up like I did.)

You may not be professing eternal love with your next slide deck, but you can win your audience's attention—maybe even some level of affection—if you put your ideas in a smart sequential order.

This linear order of *sequencing* is best married to a vertical strategy of *stratifying*—that is, designing your message so that it moves from simplicity to complexity.

Picture a pyramid with three sections, moving from top to bottom:

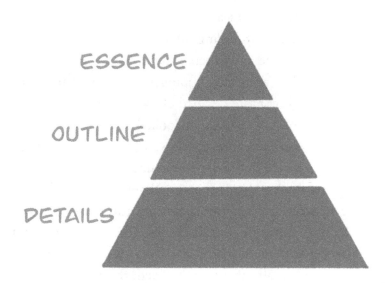

1. **Essence.** Get right to a condensed summary of the most salient point. That's the hook. Articulate the simple, distilled essence.
2. **Outline.** Follow with a brief outline, summary, or broader context. Let the reader know where the information is coming from and where it's going.
3. **Details.** Give us the rest of the information now that the brain is primed by the first two steps.

This layering—stratification—gives the audience a chance to engage progressively instead of having to sort through a bunch of confusion in the crucial early moments.

If this seems familiar, it's because consultants have been using this sort of framework for decades. It originated with the management thinker Barbara Minto, in her influential book *The Pyramid Principle*.[22]

In his years as a research analyst, Josh Bernoff learned the importance of arranging information in a logical hierarchy. Writers and presenters should start with the most important idea, then offer supporting evidence and context, followed by more detailed explanations. We don't go to a restaurant to receive an uncooked pile of raw ingredients; we're there to experience a well-prepared meal, with the courses served in the right sequence. Large information sets, in particular, demand an intelligent order. Failing to bring structure is a form of communication disrespect.

In the healthcare world, clinical study reprints use a stratifying approach. There is a brief description of the purpose and results of the study. Then, there is a synopsis/overview of the key elements of the study. The rest is all the details.

Think about how most books are structured. The distilled essence is found in the title and subtitle. The table of contents functions as an outline of the content. Then the chapters contain the details (perhaps with even deeper details using footnotes and links).

A book is a big lump of content, but this principle applies to communications of all sizes. For instance, stratifying is a far more effective way to compose emails. Get right to the point in the subject line and first sentence by articulating the relevance. Then move to short statements, explanations, and bullet points. Finally, if necessary, follow up with more detail, deeper in the body of the email, in an attachment, or via links.

Think about the difference between these two email openings:

- Subject: An update from HR on Policy B-102
- Subject: Take one minute to fill out this form by Friday (re: your paycheck)

One of those subject lines engages me immediately. The other is vague and does not let me know the point—and therefore invites me to hit the Delete key.

You never want to force your audience to work to figure out the point you're communicating. You want to hand it to them immediately so they can decide whether to engage or move on. Patience may be a virtue, but not when it comes to trying the patience of your audience.

> **You never want to force your audience to work to figure out the point you're communicating.**

> *"People are tempted to tell you everything, with perfect accuracy, right up front, when they should be giving you just enough info to be useful, then a little more, then a little more."*
> —**CHIP HEATH, *MADE TO STICK***

The progression from short to long, from simple to complex, is brain-friendly. Conversely, when you over-whelm with unstratified information, you invite the reader to tune out. Be in a hurry to highlight the value. Make the main point obvious. Go to what matters right away. The first seconds are your yellow highlighter moment.

Returning to our prior example of the sales manager coaching her field rep, she can get right to the high-value point by stating up front that "our most successful field reps over the past five years have *always* been those utilizing a pre-call planning framework. They're the ones that get President's Club awards." The point: This is what successful performance looks like.

In her book, This Isn't Working!: Evolving the Way We Work to Decrease Stress, Anxiety, and Depression,[23] career transition expert Catherine Altman Morgan underscores how many of us are exhausted and overwhelmed in this post-COVID world, with no spare energy to try to interpret what others are saying. She encourages us to picture our reader/listener as someone leaning back in their seat, skeptical, thinking "why should I care?" They are liable at a moment's notice to disengage and start scrolling or watching videos.

Now, with that picture in mind: How are you going to hook that person with an intriguing opening line in your email, resume, website, talk, or LinkedIn profile? How can you get right to the point in just a few seconds?

Speaking of pictures, why have I chosen to pepper this book with simple line drawings? Simple—I want to get to the point immediately using your visual processing system in conjunction with the written words.

I see many websites with vague, uncompelling head-lines like "Leveraging optimum end-to-end solutions to produce business results." Maybe there's a specific point of relevance somewhere on the site, but I'm not going to go digging for it. I'm clicking away.

If you've invested the time and energy to actually have a point, don't be shy about making it plain and practical. Intelligently arrange your ideas and words. Effective communication is not a game of twenty questions.

CLARITY SPOTLIGHT

"Never in the history of humanity have we vomited more words in more places with more velocity." So begins the introductory chapter (The Fog of Words) in the remarkable book, *Smart Brevity*.[24] The start-up media company Axios recognized how much time and effort was being wasted by poorly designed communications and decided to develop an approach to make information consumption more effective for news readers.

Posted on the wall in the company's lunchroom: "Brevity is confidence. Length is fear." It delivers brief summary stories in sound-bite-sized pieces. Its popular newsletters stratify and get right to the relevant point.

The founders of Axios and Politico (Jim VandeHei, Mike Allen, and Roy Schwartz) have decades of experience in media, and they concluded that condensed communication was the only way to win in an information-saturated world. Their quick-scan daily news summary style has been enormously successful because readers can focus on one important thing, then dig deeper if they so desire.

Less than six years after launching Axios, the founders sold it to Cox Enterprises for $525 million. Now that's a return on clarity!

CHAPTER 5:

You Shall Get the Point Across

"The secret to good writing is to use small words for big ideas, not to use big words for small ideas."

—OLIVER MARKUS MALLOY

Securing attention by getting to the point is a major accomplishment, but it's not the entire sequence. Next, you must embed your message in memory and make sure people clearly understand it.

Most people settle for "message sent" without realizing that the goal is actually "message received." As a communication designer, I want to reach across the void and turn the light on in your brain. That's why I (and you) need to *simplify*.

What makes this so challenging? We humans live in a complex world and have limited processing power to digest, repackage, and apply everything coming at us. There is only so much brainpower to go around.

David Rock, in his book *Your Brain at Work*[25] put it this way: "(the) ability to simplify complicated ideas into their core elements is a habit most successful executives have developed...In Hollywood, for example, the ideal pitch for a new movie is supposed to be so short that a studio can 'get' it in just one sentence. (There is a story that the movie *Alien* was pitched as *'Jaws in space'*)...When you reduce complex ideas to just a few concepts, it's far easier to manipulate the concepts in your mind, and in other people's minds."

But the issue is not just capacity, it's also shared meaning. I've already discussed the mental metadata problem, the reality that each of us has a differing understanding of words and concepts. That means you need to define, explain, and illustrate to ensure actual understanding. Related to the mental metadata challenge is the phenomenon called "The Curse of Knowledge." This is the very human tendency to assume that everyone else has the same background information in their heads as you do. You can't effectively make your point when you fail to realize that what is abundantly clear to you may be unfamiliar or confusing to your audience.

You might rush through material, use unfamiliar terms, spew jargon, or leave out crucial pieces of information that would connect the dots. This is particularly common in high-expertise environments like technology, healthcare, and engineering.

The overuse of jargon is a particular plague, especially in business communications. Josh Bernoff, in a 2017 article entitled, "Bad Writing Costs Businesses Billions,"[26] shares a compelling data point: 81 percent of businesspeople in a survey agreed with the statement, "Poorly written material wastes a lot of my time." A key time-waster is fog-filled jargon.

I can't help but laugh (or cringe) every time I see a description like, "I'm leveraging my content development skills to foster the implementation of a print-centric knowledge-transfer vehicle." Why not just say, "I'm writing a book"?

When I am coaching a business owner or consultant about their message, I ask them to try to describe what they do—and the value they bring—as if they were talking across the fence to neighbor. In a single sentence. For a 12-year-old neighbor with the attention span of a gnat.

Why don't you try that right now? You might be surprised at how complicated your everyday language has become.

Let's go back to our field sales coaching scenario. The sales manager might say to the field rep, "pre-call planning is not a nice-to-have option, like heated seats. It's your steering wheel." The comparative imagery memorably illustrates the point.

We humans have a seemingly unlimited ability to miss the message. So, here's the foundational perspective you can adopt for this step in the sequence: Assume that others can easily misunderstand you unless you simplify your words and pointedly explain your meaning. You want to try to develop two versions of your message—the technically accurate version and the dumbed-down shorthand version. That sounds a little demeaning, but it's actually one of the most considerate things you can do (as long as you don't call people dumb in the process).

> **Assume that others can easily misunderstand you unless you simplify your words and pointedly explain your meaning.**

This challenge is not confined to business. According to clinical psychologist Donald L. Davidson, PhD,[27] arriving at shared meaning between client and counselor is an essential first step in understanding a patient's unique story and moving toward accurate diagnosis and treatment. Two patients might present with self-described anxiety issues, but one might have mild symptoms based on situational stress while another might suffer frequent and debilitating panic attacks. One patient might describe suicidal ideation as a periodic passing thought, while another is seriously considering taking their life every day.

Only by asking clarifying questions can any health-care professional arrive at an accurate understanding of the problem. Assumptions about the use and meaning of certain words is risky without clarifying questions. One of the most important questions a doctor—or, really, any human being—can ask another person is, "what do you mean by that?"

Earlier in this book, I needed to explain the reticular activating system, which is a complex piece of neurobiological engineering. Here's how I explained it simply in a way you'll remember: It's the *information gatekeeper*. It's the *master filter*. It's a *bouncer at the front door*. These analogies are shortcuts to help get the point across in a more vivid and simple manner. The best communicators make liberal use of symbolic language (metaphors, analogies, comparisons, word pictures) to get their point across.

Communicating well is a form of verbal/written paint-ing. You want to create colorful images and memorable nuggets of truth in the minds of others. You want to engage the imagination and touch the emotions. "Do you see what I mean?" becomes an important question as you design your communications.

In Part 3, we'll outline eight powerful common short-cuts (tools) that will help you simplify and explain your meaning in a brain-friendly fashion.

CLARITY SPOTLIGHT

Author Bob Goff is a master of storytelling and vivid imagery. He uses catchy and amusing chapter titles like, "Do A Cannonball With Your Life—It's Okay To Get A Little Wet" and "Every Time We See People As Ordinary, We Turn The Wine Back Into Water."

In his book, **Live in Grace, Walk in Love**, he says "I find most of the big Christian words thrown around in some faith communities distracting, so I don't use them. I try to speak as plainly as I can so I can understand what I mean, and so everyone else around me can, too."[28]

Exactly. Just swap out "Christian" and "faith" with any other sub-group and the principle applies. Engineers. Programmers. Clinicians. In any endeavor when you and others go deep into technical details, it's easy to become immersed in tribal jargon.

I got caught breaking this rule in a recent clarity workshop that I was giving. Ironically, I was talking about how others had me confused in a meeting years ago by throwing around a common acronym that I didn't know yet—and I, the relative newcomer, felt lost. Been there before?

Then someone raised her hand in my session and asked me what that particular acronym meant. I had assumed everyone in the room knew! Oops.

CHAPTER 6:

You Shall Get
on the Same Page

"If it's not written, it never happened.
If it is written, it doesn't matter what happened."
—SERCAN LEYLEK

Here's a rule to live by: If you don't document an agreement in words, you're just looking for trouble. You've probably heard the common expression, "A verbal contract isn't worth the paper it's written on." You need to nail things down. In writing.

In a word: *solidify*.

It's a common expression in selling (and teaching):

- Tell them what you're going to tell them.
- Tell them.
- Tell them what you told them.

People tend to listen in bits and pieces, and they often don't put all the pieces together. So do your audience a favor by employing:

1. Repetition—make major points more than one time, in more than one way.
2. Conclusion—be explicit about application; don't assume correct implications or deductions.
3. Summarization—draw together the information and conclusions in an easy-to-remember format.

In sales, people learn about ABC (Always Be Closing). The best practice in all forms of communication is ABS (Always Be Solidifying).

As a speaker, I have worked on my material for many hours, so I am carrying around the flow, the progression, and the implications in my head. The audience, however, isn't. That means I'm responsible for providing clear and simple conclusions, suggestions, applications, and quick-hit summaries.

Many of my colleagues in the training field provide not only bodies of content, but also reinforcement and summary tools to make sure audiences remember and apply the training.

This brings to mind an amusing line from *The Princess Bride* (again, from Inigo Montoya). As the protagonists are about to storm the castle, Inigo says, "Let me explain. No, there is too much. Let me sum up." Great advice for millions of businesspeople!

During my many years working with corporate clients on their collaborative projects, one of the most common (and painful) experiences was the struggle to get everyone to agree—on anything.

Really agree. On goals. On scope. On timelines. On process. On budget. On expectations. All those pesky details.

Here's what would happen at the kickoff of a project, for instance. Some or all core team members meet to discuss that project. Things are said. Discussion ensues. Heads nod. Long email strings begin to proliferate. The parties assume that agreement has occurred, and the project moves forward.

A month later, an early deliverable shows up, and the howling begins. It turns out that the picture wasn't actually clear to all team members. The VP thought it would look like this other thing. The vendor had a different idea of the end goal. The project manager was fuzzy on the details. To top it all off, the legal reviewer now questions whether this initiative can even pass muster. Team members had not solidified the scope, process, and intent.

Why? Because nobody created the "same page." Agreement was left floating in the air, instead of being fixed on paper (or in a digital file).

The Bible is a very big book with a lot of details. Luckily for Moses, the ten commandments distilled the key moral responsibilities for Israel. Carved in stone. The bottom line, as it were, that all the other details rolled up to.

Then, centuries later, Jesus of Nazareth provided an even simpler distillation of *that* summary. He boiled down the point of the entire Mosaic Law into two core principles: love God and love your neighbor. Detailed documentation is important; but, by and large, people can only remember and apply brief, memorable summaries.

> *"Every time I stand to communicate, I want to take one simple truth and lodge it in the heart of the listener. I want them to know that one thing and know what to do with it."*
>
> **—ANDY STANLEY**

The best leaders are masters of summary. They know their teams cannot possibly hold all the details or see the bigger picture, so sketching it out in brief verbal and written snapshots is how you can move more readily to desired change and action.

You should always assume your audience has not connected all the pieces or seen many of the implications. By giving them something quick and simple, you increase the chance that they will absorb and remember the message.

> ## The most effective way to get people on the "same page" is a written summary.

The most effective way to get people on the "same page" is a written summary. You can create it as a distilled brand statement or incorporate it as part of a detailed project plan—either way, document and share it. Alignment and agreement need to occur based on clearly articulated solidifying statements: goals, purpose statements, executive summaries, scope descriptions, and step-by-step plans.

Corporate lawyers—who, let's face it, are often full of long-winded complexity—will never go out of style. Why? Because we need thoughtful written summaries, agreements, and contracts. They make the solidifying documents that articulate agreement. That's where clarity and accountability stem from.

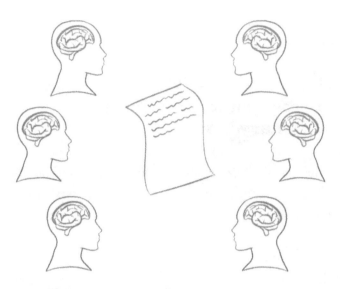

After her field coaching visit, the sales manager in our ongoing story should send a brief, pointed email to her sales rep detailing the exact steps she expects to see enacted for future sales calls. This written summary is the basis for ongoing development and accountability.

Getting on the same page is a huge issue in business. Some documents don't solidify anything because they are vague and non-specific. Here is where I see some of the most common gaps:

- Purpose statements (vision, mission, values) that are utterly generic and nonactionable.
- Job/role descriptions that are too vague to create day-to-day alignment of expectations between team members and managers.
- Project plans that are too general to provide a clear roadmap for all stakeholders.

- Teams with poorly defined roles and responsibilities.
- Sales messages that are ill-defined across representatives, managers, and sales leaders.

Untold millions of dollars are lost every year due to a lack of simple summaries. Dale Carnegie (author of *How to Win Friends and Influence People*) put it this way: "Ninety percent of all management problems are caused by miscommunication." That's frightening but also fixable.

One of the most high-impact summaries that companies neglect to create are departmental and team purpose statements. High-level company purpose statements are great if they are well composed and actionable. In reality, however, each *division* of the company also has its own identity, purpose, and goals, and needs written summaries. Leaders need to articulate and reinforce these. Solidifying team cohesion and culture depends on having simple, memorable statements that inform direction and effort.

Have a point. Get to the point. Get the point across. Get on the same page. Practicing these four simple rules will revolutionize your communication.

How might these four steps unfold in a practical scenario? Let's say you're heading up a board meeting for a nonprofit organization. You get to be the cat-herder for ten diverse people with just three hours to make some major fund-raising decisions.

1. **What's the point?** Outline, up-front, the final decision(s) that need to come out of this meeting.

That is the deliverable from your time together. Make the goal explicit and specific—the point "B" in the A-to-B Shift. Insist that this meeting *is not for* free-flowing brainstorms or getting into the weeds, but this discussion *is for* reaching agreement and alignment on an action plan.

2. **Get to the point.** Open the meeting by handing out a blank summary template and explain that success looks like having this document completed in the first two hours, with final decisions to be made in the third hour.

3. **Get the point across.** Ensure that all ten people have a common understanding of terms as you discuss ideas and wording, and ask individuals to define what they mean when they use specific words (especially more technical financial concepts).

4. **Get on the same page.** Summarize the results of the meeting, including the filled-in template, in an email that locks down (in writing) what everyone is aligning to as they approach the next phase of planning.

In sequence, these four steps help keep your communication design focused and effective. You're pursuing results, not just spending time shooting the breeze.

Great leaders set the tone, listen, and consolidate, but ultimately, they are responsible for decisions and leadership—they must summarize and solidify. Even if there is not 100 percent consensus on all points, there needs to be a clear and agreed-upon road map.

CLARITY SPOTLIGHT

There are so many failed projects—and not because anyone has bad intentions. Often, there is simply a lack of project management and collaboration skills.

In 2006, I started my life sciences consultancy (Impactiviti) because I saw a major unmet need for better relationships between training departments and outside vendor/partners. In the ten years prior, working on the vendor side, I saw how many of these relationships went sideways because of a bad client/vendor "fit" joined with poor communications practices.

Many of the vendors did not have a clear direction and differentiating brand, so part of Impactiviti's practice was brand strategy and messaging.

But many people on the client side of the equation never had any project management training because they had come into their roles from field sales positions. This indicated a need for hands-on upskilling workshops focused on collaborative communications.[29]

The overriding concept throughout the entire workshop is this: Be proactive and do not assume anything. Get everyone informed and on the same page.

While we initially focused on practical project management workshops, it soon became clear that the core principles applied to all sorts of corporate collaboration. Getting the point across and getting on the same page involves a set of skills we all need.

Part 3:

The Clarity Fuel Formula Tools

One of the biggest nightmares for the Allied forces in World War 2 was the German Enigma cipher machine.

Enigma was an ingenious system for coding and decoding military messages. It's been estimated that 158,962,555,217,826,360,000 combinations of characters were possible (give or take a few) when using the Enigma Machine, and the Germans changed the key for deciphering messages nightly, making it a nearly impossible code to crack.

The gripping story of how a brilliant group of British intellectuals cracked the Enigma code (and advanced the science of digital computing we so rely on today) was portrayed in the excellent 2014 film, *The Imitation Game*, featuring actor Benedict Cumberbatch as Alan Turing.

Secret codes are all about misdirection and fog. Anyone working on decoding Enigma desperately wanted a shortcut. It took Alan Turing's genius to find the key.

What was the purpose of Enigma? In a word, to *obfuscate*. To obscure the message. To overtax the brain. To make it as hard as possible for anyone tapping into the broadcast signals to make any sense of them.

You don't want your communications to be enigmatic. You don't want your words to be like a disorienting verbal snowstorm, leaving others lost and discouraged. Instead of hiding the keys to our meaning, you want to hand the keys out liberally.

Anyone can create a long, run-on set of sentences. Expansion is not the skill you need for success. Distillation is. Simplification is. Woodrow Wilson once said, "If it is a ten-minute speech it takes me all of two weeks to prepare it; if it is a half-hour speech it takes me a week; if I can talk as long as I want to it requires no preparation at all. I am ready now."

The human brain reacts well to certain forms of word packages: shortcuts that quickly turn the lights on. Sound bites that grab attention. Simplifiers that paint a picture. I will show you eight shortcuts (statements, snippets, specifics, stories, stakes, symbols, side-by-sides, summaries) you can employ to get your point across quickly and memorably.

CHAPTER 7:

Statements

"To get your ideas across, use small words,
big ideas and short sentences."
—JOHN HENRY PATTERSON

The opening of the ancient book of Genesis is one whale of a statement: "In the beginning God created the heavens and the earth."

The Bible is a big book, brimming with big ideas and mind-bending narratives. But it is also filled with unmistakably plain and straightforward statements, including that monster introductory declaration about all of life, creation, and history.

You might doubt the veracity of it, but there can be no doubt that this is an incredibly clear statement, one that has informed faith and sparked debate for millennia.

A statement is an assertion or declaration that expresses a fact, opinion, or idea. It is a sentence or phrase that is either true or false, and its purpose is to pointedly communicate information or express a thought or belief. Ideally, you should be able to distill an idea into a brief, simple sentence. It's a sound bite that the brain can process immediately.

Political leaders are often experts in obfuscation, but some of our most memorable statements came from those who had a single, vital point to make:

- "We hold these truths to be self-evident, that all men are created equal."—Thomas Jefferson
- "I came, I saw, I conquered."—Julius Caesar

A statement is not vague, and it's not ambiguous. Statements say one thing well and waste no words. They're meant to be processed instantly and remembered easily.

Statements say one thing well and waste no words. They're meant to be processed instantly and remembered easily.

"X is the biggest threat to our democracy today!" You've heard and read such sound-bite declarations hundreds of times, especially in the run-up to an election. To stand out in a crowded field, politicians and reporters must become skilled at condensing big ideas into simple, vivid word packages.

It could take anywhere from several paragraphs to a full-scale book to completely explain why and how *x* is such an existential threat to our democracy. It would be more detailed and nuanced to say, "Among the dozens of suboptimal forces coming to bear on the health of our national life (including this, that, and the other thing), it is my considered opinion, and that of most of my senior advisors, that our first priority should be to ameliorate the effects of *x*, which is creating significant issues for many citizens, blah, blah, blah."

But that long format won't jar the brain awake and implant a memory. It's not switching the lights on; it's just adding to the clutter. Voluminous vague verbiage is not RAS-friendly. You need a shortcut to wrap it up.

This principle applies to every realm, not just politics. Businesses can easily fall into the trap of spewing out technical jargon that sounds important but is really nothing more than a plague of vague.

The website for Blue Spoon Consulting[30] delivers this hot mess of forgettable jargon: "The New World Disorder is a place where strategic shock, multi-dimensional dysfunctionality and exponential change interact and entangle so completely that the Standard Model of thought and inaction won't...doesn't...can't work as a compass to navigate a different moment. The era of linear solutioning is over."

Ugh. Sorry...I'm feeling a bit dizzy. If words can cause headaches, that bunch is serving up a migraine. Instead, a brief phrase like, "what got you here isn't going to get you there," would be a nice, simple statement to summarize a need for new thinking.

Branding and high-level purpose statements are great starting points. However, in your daily workflow, you can condense your message into simple statements as well. What is the specific goal of this sales call? How would I summarize the point of this slide? What one-sentence statement describes the purpose of this meeting? What is the actual point and desired result of this email?

Think of statements as simple, declarative nuggets. Here's an easy trick to help you compose them: Start with the phrase (best silently mouthed in a southern accent) "Well, I declare,..." and then finish with an assertion. No clauses, no nuances, no explanations. Now you have a forthright statement that the audience can definitively understand and react to.

(Pro tip: Before delivering the message, be sure to remove the "Well, I declare,..." part.)

Once you can put your communications into short statements for yourself, you can then do it for your audience.

(Well, I declare) *Every type of communication should be fueled by succinct, punchy statements.* Look back at the sentence in italics you just finished reading. Yep—just like that.

What's your high-level purpose? What's your message in a given situation? When you package your intentions into a simple statement, you're allowing your audience (the hard-working brain) to get the point—immediately.

"Writing long sentences is like adding water to tea; the more words, the weaker the message," wrote Dianna Booher. Brief and clear statements are highly effective. But sometimes we just want one potato chip out of the bag. So, let's look at a portion that can be even smaller...

CHAPTER 8:

Snippets

"If you can't explain something in a few words,
try fewer."

—ROBERT BREAULT

Fact: Australia is wider than the moon.

Seriously. Never would have guessed. The moon is 3,400 kilometers in diameter, while Australia (from east to west) is nearly 4,000 kilometers. Striking fact, memorably stated. I may never look at a world map the same way again.

That interesting piece of information could have been explained in a convoluted and boring fashion, but a great snippet is all about brain-friendly brevity. Your listener can only allocate a tiny memory space for you—what seed do you want to plant there?

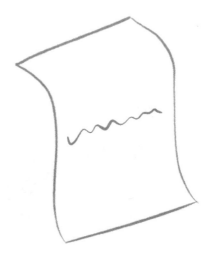

A snippet is a short excerpt of something larger. It might be a factoid, an example, a keyword, a statistic, a quote—even a part of a song lyric. It's a sneaky little piece of information that the brain cannot help but seize on. Snippets are the sound bites of sound bites, turning on the light in the brain and carrying an oversized payload of impact.

- "I have a dream."—Martin Luther King Jr. (a key snippet of a longer speech).
- The richest person in the world is _____ (this factoid keeps changing, so I'm going to leave the punch line blank).
- "All you need is love"—song title (and chorus) by the Beatles.
- The Mars Rover Opportunity, designed to be active for 90 days, remained functional for more than 15 years.

Snippets are the sound bites of sound bites, turning on the brain light and carrying an oversized payload of impact.

Effective presenters use snippets all the time when designing their slides. The snippets may be words, numbers, memes, or illustrative images, but what they have in common is they get a point into the audience's brain—fast.

Pithy branding taglines are great examples of snippets.

- "Just do it"—Nike
- "Think different"—Apple
- "Eat fresh"—Subway
- "The world on time"—FedEx
- "The ultimate driving machine"—BMW
- "Ideas worth spreading"—TED
- "The Happiest Place on Earth"—Disneyland

"Your main competitor is the noise" is a phrase I often use that contains a snippet. Because it's surprising and relevant, it sticks. Why do you need to apply clarity principles for effective communication design? In a snippet: #Noise.

Educator Angela Maiers inspires audiences (teachers, students, and others) with a simple and powerful two-word snippet: You Matter. It's a tiny phrase that powers a movement.

"Doctor, this new medication has been shown to be 34 percent more effective than the standard of care at the six-month mark." Sure, there are plenty of charts and graphs and research details that support that claim, but the pharmaceutical representative needs to pull out the most vital snippet (34 percent more effective) to implant the message.

Whatever you might think about Donald Trump, he has always been a master marketer. MAGA (Make America Great Again) was a highly effective snippet that burrowed deeply into the minds of millions, whether they liked it or not. A similarly effective acronym—one I've agreed with ever since first hearing it—is the KISS principle: Keep It Simple, Stupid.

Speaking of stupid, James Carville hit it out of the park with one summary election campaign snippet in 1992: "It's the economy, stupid." Untold thousands of words are expended in any national campaign, but one memorable snippet can rise above all that noise and embed itself in the mind.

Visual snippets possess unique power. Packaging a message into a striking visual can get the point across instantly, because, as the saying goes, a picture is worth a thousand words. I stopped ordering Starbucks Frappuccinos some years back because of one visual I came across, showing the shocking amount of sugar in the drink. Instant conviction and motivation to action.

Social media platforms like Twitter and TikTok have flourished because, in our era of endless stimulation and short attention spans, snippets rule.

Even if you don't have the creative gift of composing taglines, you can easily become a master at using snippets others have published. Your best friend for finding snippets is a search engine.

You can take any topic and search for appropriate facts, quotes, statistics, and phrases. There is also an endless array of images and memes to stir up ideas. Just be sure you practice fact-checking and attribution if you use someone else's snippets.

Let's say you have a paragraph's worth of content to share. Look at all of those words and ask yourself, "what is the main point here?" Then put that into a single sentence. Now go further—can you reduce that nugget into a pithy phrase?

Why are snippets effective? Because, like a single M&M, they're small and easy to consume. They get to the point and take up little memory space. Using snippets effectively is our way of recognizing that every member of our audience has very limited bandwidth for new information. So, you package up your message with little nuggets that can "stick."

Snippets (which can also be short statements and specifics) are potent bits of information that stick easily in the human mind.

CLARITY SPOTLIGHT
—SANDY WOODRUFF

For some strange reason, one of my favorite words has always been "discombobulation." It's fun just to say it. What does it mean? Messy chaos.

Well, one day I wondered—if discombobulation is a word, starting with a prefix, then surely the word "combobulation" must exist. Makes sense, right? Well, it does, and it means exactly what you think—creating order out of chaos. (In fact, Milwaukee Wisconsin's airport has sections just beyond the security checkpoints called "Recombobulation Areas," and that is my favorite piece of airport signage in the world!)

The light went on. I don't normally recommend that anyone "brand" their spouse, but I told my wife that this one keyword accurately distills her makeup. She has always created order out of any chaos, personal or professional. An organizer extraordinaire. She is, in fact, the Combobulator. That's memorable personal clarity summarized in a single snippet.

We're not planning to create a business out of combobulation—just acknowledging the very orderly environment here at home—but the fact is, clarity principles carry over into every sphere of life, including knowing your own personal strengths and DNA.

CHAPTER 9:

Specifics

"The more specific we are, the more universal something can become. Life is in the details. If you generalize, it doesn't resonate. The specificity of it is what resonates."

—JACQUELINE WOODSON

Our minds are far more inclined to tune in to specifics rather than generalities. Specifics are particulars that are explicit and well defined. Specifics may be names, numbers, places, dates, details, examples. Specifics lead to recall, to differentiation, to well-defined action.

Particulars stick. Generalities are forgettable.

| **Particulars stick.** |
| **Generalities are forgettable.** |

Which of these two individuals is more likely to get a well-targeted job interview or referral?

- *"Seeking a new role in business operations management."*
- *"Ideally suited to help the leaders of a growing early-stage software development company scale to the next level by managing a team of internal and outsourced technical developers."*

If your LinkedIn profile claims that you are a highly valued member of the sales team—ho-hum. If you can claim, however, that you've exceeded 110 percent of quota for three straight years, and you ranked in the top five nationally—that's specific. Now I'm listening.

"These advanced new double-pane windows are proven to reduce your heating bill by 22 percent annually." I may forget all the technical details about the window design, but I will latch on to that specific selling point. Numbers have teeth.

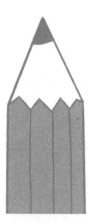

If a newspaper quoted general statistics about the life expectancy and exercise habits of people my age, I'll likely yawn and move on—even when there's something very important for me to hear. However, if a childhood friend tells me that so-and-so from my high school class unexpectedly dropped dead of a heart attack due to obesity last Thursday in downtown Hartford—now I'm engaged. And I'm more likely to change my ways. Details turn generalities into realities. Sharpen your pencil to make a more precise impression.

Consultant and business owner Kim M. Catania describes[31] working with one company where the principal could not get out of the clouds of big-picture vision and bring the discussion down to specific deliverables. She had to take all that high-level conceptualizing and translate it into a suggested specific application, at a tangible level, for approval and execution. This is a very common business challenge that happens when people don't tell us exactly what they want, how they want it, and when it needs to be completed.

This underscores the need in our interactions with partners and clients to: Be clear. Be direct. Be meaningful. Be specific.

If you're going to be great at using specifics, the keyword you'll train yourself to keep top-of-mind is "exactly." Exactly how much, how many, how often? Exactly what results transpired? Exactly how was that done, and how should it be done in the future? Exactly what is expected of me in this job? What, exactly, do you mean by that?

Being specific is crucial in business messaging (and strategy). I've gone through some variation of this exchange countless times with companies and consultants to get beyond generalities:

- *What's your target audience?* Large corporations.
- *OK, exactly how large is large when it comes to employee count and annual revenue?* Most of my clients have more than 3,000 employees and generate more than $1 billion in revenue.
- *Are your clients primarily local, national, global, or something else?* North America only.
- *Exactly which divisions or departments purchase your offering?* Mostly HR, though some manufacturing compliance groups also value what we do.
- *What's the typical title of your decision-maker?* Mainly VP or senior director, though we often have an entry point with lower-level managers.
- *What exactly is your clients' biggest source of business pain?* After companies reach a certain threshold of size, their cobbled-together methods of automation are falling apart. They want one cohesive system.
- *What's the primary selling point these decision-makers value above all else?* Rapid implementation with our hosted technology platform.

You see the point. A salesperson or marketer needs these specifics to target efforts. A potential referral partner needs to know your exact sweet spot in the market. And in all communications, the more precise and specific the messaging, the more likely the point will resonate.

No one can execute on vagueness. It is not helpful to leave people guessing and deciphering intent. It wasn't a leap of logic for Kim Catania to compare these situations with needing to use specifics to interact with teenagers under your roof. "Clean your entire room before bedtime tonight or you won't be able to use the car tomorrow."

Managers and other leaders can set their people up for success only by giving memorable and visualizable particulars: precise targets, tangible expectations, specific and measurable goals, and clear-cut expected behaviors. Specifics are some of your best tools to rise above our VUCA environment.

The human brain will latch on to specifics. But there's something else that we humans absolutely love (even from childhood), and it is one of your most powerful tools to get your ideas across to others.

CHAPTER 10:

Stories

Everyone knows that the human brain is hardwired for stories. Before the printing press (and the Internet), people passed down knowledge orally. Storytelling is the art of conveying a narrative or series of events through spoken or written language, often with the aim of entertaining, educating, or inspiring an audience.

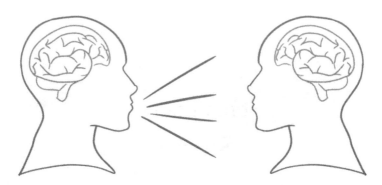

Stories generally include a beginning, middle, and end. They follow a narrative arc that includes a conflict or challenge, a rising action or reaction, a climax, and a resolution.

Stories "stick" far more effectively than facts. Facts can be quite sterile, but stories wrap truth in vivid, human, relatable terms. Stories paint pictures in the imagination and lodge in the memory.

Storytelling is a crucial component for effective sales, leadership, public speaking, long-form writing, professional networking; you name it, every form of communication is enhanced by using stories.

Every form of communication is enhanced by using stories.

When a US president gives a State of the Union address, they usually weave stories of individuals into the speech, along with the usual assortment of facts, falsehoods, statistics, and promises. Individuals and their stories end up being more memorable than pronouncements, because we can relate to the people (who are frequently pointed out in the audience).

I often tell the story about how I went to Vanderbilt University so I could study astronomy. I love all things about space. But then I ran head-on into calculus and physics, and my aspiration turned quickly into science fiction. I hate formulas. I was a Physics Phailure—so it was time to pivot (to psychology, as it turned out).

I could just say, "I majored in psychology," but isn't the minor disaster of my story more memorable? Because there's humanity in the tale—we can all relate to making course changes.

The best-selling book ever—the Bible—is a series of memorable and striking stories, which tell a grand meta-narrative. The story of young David taking on the Philistine giant Goliath with just a sling and a stone is an underdog narrative for which many people have felt an affinity throughout the ages. This enduring lesson is one of the reasons that my favorite sports moment of all time was when a team of upstart US college students defeated the mighty Soviet hockey team in the 1980 Lake Placid Winter Olympics and went on to win the gold medal. To this day, the story still gives me goose bumps.

There are many forms of stories that you can apply to get your point across to others:

- **Origin story**—how the company (or the individual) started on this quest.
- **Evolution story**—what happened along the way to bring you to this point.

- **Success story**—a personal anecdote that illustrates an important point showing why you/your company provides value or fits in a certain way.
- **Comeback story**—the protagonist sinks into defeat and then rises again to victory and success.
- **Case study**—stories about how people accomplished something.
- **How-to stories**—a step-by-step account of how to accomplish a certain thing.
- **Hero's journey story**—wrapping up a lesson or perspective in the familiar narrative of hero versus obstacle or bad guy.

Every organization can craft a variety of these stories to help engage clients, donors, partners, and media outlets.

A powerful form of story is a testimonial (which is a brief case study focusing on what someone did for a customer). Here's a simple structure anyone can use to craft a brief testimonial:

1. **Problem:** I was experiencing this important need/problem/pain/challenge.
2. **Reason:** I reached out to Diana Smith because x (often, it's because someone else you trusted made the recommendation).
3. **Experience:** What I learned/experienced was this positive, beneficial thing that has made a significant difference.
4. **Outcome:** Now I'm doing this differently or have experienced this benefit, growth, or tangible result.

I asked one of my clients, a marketing director with one of the world's largest insurance providers (MetLife), to write up such a testimonial[32] using this format:

> I work in a complex industry, so it's incredibly challenging to craft communications that are clear enough to be impactful and yet comprehensive enough to relay the full message. My team was experiencing this tension every day, and we were determined to find a better way.
>
> A trusted mentor recommended I connect with Steve Woodruff, and midway through our first conversation, I knew he could help us.
>
> After Steve's three-day training, my team reassessed the clarity of our materials and began using proven tools and techniques to improve them. The team was most struck by the idea of memory darts and the need to fight against ambiguous language (it's harder than it sounds). Steve's style made the lessons memorable—his mental shortcuts, quick lists, humor, and examples ensured that, months later, we still recall the learnings and can apply them easily.
>
> We even have an amusing metric that we apply to our materials—what would the KoC (King of Clarity) think?
>
> What surprised me most is that now my team is much better able to articulate why simplifying our communications is so important to influence stakeholders for greater results. I'm thrilled to see our marketing assets driving more meaningful conversations and leading up to a number of wins early in our season.

Stories with lessons, such as Aesop's Fables, remain eternally popular because they encapsulate truths growing out of the tension and flow of a memorable narrative. Why should we be careful about being purveyors of fear and doom? Well, because of the boy who cried wolf.

Comedians can make a fine living by telling stories. Stories with an amusing twist are what win audiences, because whether or not we can relate to the actual story (usually we do), just the act of storytelling is mesmerizing and memorable.

Stories are amazing tools, but the most engaging story is yours. You may be one of a million companies or one of eight billion individuals, but your story is unique. Your life narrative is a critical part of your personal brand. Here's a simple template you, as an individual, can use to craft your career story:

- I started here (might be childhood, school, first job, or first role in a specific company).
- Then, this happened (some kind of significant change or person who made an impact).
- Now, I'm doing this (current role/job).
- The direction I am heading in is (future aspiration).

A similar outline can be used to tell a company origin/evolution story.

Stories are amazing tools, but the most engaging story is yours.

When you can tell others—and yourself—the story arc of your journey, you are far more likely to be remembered for the right reasons and receive targeted referrals.

In the first chapter of this book, I told a story about a Russian oligarch and his ill-fated chateau project. Now, I could have given a detailed explanation of various project management principles, but that particular story (which vividly sums up and illustrates those principles) stuck in your mind. You'll never forget it.

CHAPTER 11:

Stakes

"Big stories need human stakes."
—AARON SWARTZ

There are several types of questions that you can use to ask, "What are the stakes?", including: "Why does this matter?", "Why should I pay attention, remember, and act?", "What if this or that happens?"

Stakes refer to what is at risk or what you can gain (or lose) as a result of a particular action or decision. Nobody pays to see a low-wire act of some guy holding his pole and balancing while walking one inch off the ground.

Neutral, meaningless information is not what we're looking for. You watch *Top Gun* or *Mission Impossible* movies for the high-stakes drama. A two-hour film of Tom Cruise doing his laundry? Maybe not so memorable. Wrinkled shirts are not high stakes.

We want relevance with some teeth in it, some tension. "What good result will occur if I take this action? What potentially awful result might occur if I don't act?" Our brains can't help but constantly evaluate importance. It's part of our survival programming. We are always trying to evaluate what's at stake in any given circumstance.

If there is little risk or immediacy, I won't act. If there are potentially major repercussions, I'm going to make it a priority.

> **If there is little risk or immediacy, I won't act. If there are potentially major repercussions, I'm going to make it a priority.**

Why was the COVID-19 pandemic panic so widespread? Because leaders and health professionals created the perception that the stakes—for every individual, country, even the world—couldn't be higher. The end of the world as we know it—due to viruses, climate change, or tyrannical government—is a message that is always going to break through the noise.

Marketers and salespeople know that one of their biggest challenges is creating a sense of urgency. Act before midnight tonight, and you'll get these three bonuses. Buy before the end of the month, or you'll miss this discount. Your comfortable retirement may be in danger. Take this medicine, or you'll die (Okay, maybe leave that level of starkness to the attending physician).

Teachers who care about their students know that future success depends greatly on the habits they develop in their youth. So do parents, pastors, and teachers. Telling stories about opportunities lost (or gained) due to specific actions is a way of bringing clarity to minds often absorbed only with the here and now.

Do you want to see how a high-stakes topic affects people? When a topic like gun control comes up, the urgent stakes of life and death, defense and freedom, crime and tragedy all come into play. The brain and heart are engaged. A low-stakes chat about bird feeders won't generate the same level of stimulation (unless, that is, you're one of those incredibly dedicated birdwatchers).

What's at stake for you? For your department? For your customers or patients? For the company? What's at stake for the future of your community or the nation? Of course, this kind of appeal can be abused, but we have every reason to explain truly and realistically to people what hinges on their actions and decisions so that they are more inclined to remember and act.

And remember—what's at stake in the abstract ("businesses around the globe could potentially lose $1 trillion per year!") has nowhere near the emotional impact of something that directly impacts the audience ("your average employee is losing five productive hours per week due to poorly organized meetings.")

Inertia is the enemy of change. You have something important to say. Tell people why it matters, just as I'm telling you in this book why effective communication is so vital to your success.

(So: If you *don't* apply this principle, you might end up as a terrible communicator and get fired. The stakes are high!).

CHAPTER 12:

Symbols

"One good analogy is worth three hours discussion."
—DUDLEY FIELD MALONE

S ome years ago, a friend wrote on my Facebook timeline, "Happy birthday to the King of Clarity!" That was genius-level verbal shorthand, and I quickly adopted it as my brand.

It felt pretentious to adopt such a bold professional nickname, but it was unbeatable symbolic language. Brief, striking, and memorable. A bit amusing. My never-bombastic mother was quite dubious, but I ran with it anyway, because, well, who doesn't want to stand out in the minds of others as the potentate of something?

I was right. She's no longer around to hear me say it, so I guess I don't have to go to bed without supper.

Using figurative, illustrative speech means employing language that goes beyond the literal meaning of the words to create a vivid and imaginative description or comparison. It involves using figures of speech, such as metaphors, similes, personification, hyperbole, and symbolism, to convey ideas or emotions in a more creative and engaging way.

Symbolic language can wrap multiple meanings into a few vivid words—sometimes even a single word. That's the ultimate shortcut for painting a picture in the mind of another person. Why? Because symbols play off something very powerful already existing in our brains: a memory hook.

> **Symbols play off something very powerful already existing in our brains: a memory hook.**

It's hard to plant a brand-new concept in someone else's mind. It's much easier, and more efficient, to riff off an existing idea and make a link.

When Jesus wanted to explain the nature of faith, he compared it to a mustard seed—very small starting out, but eventually turning into a large, spreading plant. This was one of many symbols he used to enlighten his mostly agrarian listeners.

When you say that something is the "Lexus of x," you are implying luxury, quality, exclusivity, and a high price tag. When you tell others that "Laura comes into the room like a category 4 hurricane," we know that Laura is a social force of nature, not a reserved introvert.

One of the easiest ways to depict a large and powerful entity (think Microsoft, Google, Amazon, or Walmart) is to use the phrase "800-pound gorilla." No need for further explanation because the listener immediately understands the concept.

If you work in a more technical industry, and it's difficult to communicate what exactly you do to your neighbor, your children—or even your customer—sometimes the most direct way is through a well-chosen comparison. I know people who can describe themselves this way: "You know about those sherpas who guide climbers up Mount Everest? I'm like that—a career navigator and advisor, and my customers are marketers in career transition."

Clinical training pro Alison Quinn[33] mentions a subject matter expert who used analogies to make a complicated scientific topic easier for others to understand. She painted a verbal picture of analogy of a hematologic (blood) cancer, describing the abnormal cells as teenagers. The cells "looked like" adult, fully functional cells, but they didn't operate like responsible adults—they ran wild. Another analogy described how these cells tended to multiply quickly and out of control. She also made the connection to planting mint in a garden and how quickly it could take over the entire space.

One of the many fascinating local professionals I've met during my time in Franklin coffee shops is Andrew. He helps music artists sell their songs and catalogs to interested investors. It's one of those many niche businesses that takes some time to figure out, but after explaining the nuts and bolts, he made it easy for me to grasp by saying, "I'm essentially a real estate broker for music." Bingo. The use of the familiar to explain the unfamiliar.

One of the most important considerations to keep in mind when you use symbolic language to describe yourself or your company is to keep the language positive and aspirational. You undermine your position as a specialized purveyor of knowledge or services if you say you're a "jack of all trades," even if there is an element of truth to that.

It might be accurate to describe your driven work approach as a "bull in a china shop," but who'd want that person on the team? Better to refer to the 1980 Olympic US ice hockey team (or some other underdog) and say that "there's no quit in me, no matter what the odds."

Becoming proficient at using symbolic language means continually asking yourself, "What is this like?", or "What's a real-life picture of this?", or "How would I help a 10-year-old make the leap from the known to the new?"

Symbolic language can wrap multiple meanings into a few vivid words. It's the ultimate shortcut for painting a picture in the mind of another person.

CHAPTER 13:

Side-by-Sides

"Imagination that compares and contrasts with what is around (as well as what is better and worse) is the living power and prime agent of all human perception, judgement, and emotional reaction."

—SAMUEL TAYLOR COLERIDGE

One of the most helpful ways you can help people understand ideas is to line them up with other concepts. Compare. Contrast. This, not that. Similarities and dissimilarities.

When you explain what something is by lining it up next to something else, you make the leap of understanding much easier.

- He's as talented at golf as Tiger Woods ever was.
- This pastry puts Cinnabon to shame.
- What you're reading right now is not a long-winded business theory book; (by contrast) it's a practical handbook.
- Your prior vendor was understaffed, but our company has twenty-five FTEs ready to provide subject matter expertise.
- I want the car color to be stop-sign red, not deep maroon.
- They have big-company resources but a start-up culture.

When you explain what something is by lining it up next to something else, you make the leap of understanding much easier.

When making a comparison, you should first identify the similarities between the subjects being compared, followed by their differences. For contrast, you should focus on identifying the differences between the subjects being contrasted, followed by their similarities. In both cases, it is important to provide specific examples to clarify your points to the reader.

I had some recent trips to Wyoming, Idaho, and Montana, and as beautiful as those areas are, something kept making me feel uncomfortable. Finally, I landed on it. By contrast to the hills and forests I always felt comfortable with, the Big Sky territory was too wide open. I constantly felt exposed, like reverse-claustrophobia.

One of the unspoken questions in everyone's mind when meeting someone is going to be, "Where do you fit?" As a consultant, I constantly let people know what kinds of clients I work for and what kinds I don't, what services I do perform and what I don't do. If I want to illuminate their minds with a shortcut, I draw such comparative distinctions. Every company and brand should do the same to help potential customers quickly locate them in the right memory space.

Two of the more valuable occasions for this approach are job interviews and networking meetings. "My strength is not in being a functional manager; instead, I impart vision and seek to break new ground." "I do my best work as a solo contributor, not a cog in a large wheel." I am not this, I am that. I do this and not that.

In written or presentation materials, charts, graphs, tables, and infographics are prime tools for comparing and contrasting specific points. A great this-versus-that visual can generate instant insight without a lot of words.

A powerful application of this principle, especially for sales and marketing, is positioning yourself or your company against a "bad guy." Every good story or movie needs an enemy to contrast with the protagonist. It's far easier to sell your company's services if you position it against the Big Bad Incumbent, which is (let's say) impersonal, unresponsive, and expensive. You can tap into the emotions of your listener if you contrast yourself with a Darth Vader or Sauron in your industry.

Speaking of which, the ultimate side-by-side advertising initiative was the Pepsi challenge, where tasters blindly tasted Coke and Pepsi and had to choose which soda they preferred. Similarly, for many years, Avis positioned itself against market leader Hertz by claiming, "We're #2. We Try Harder." People naturally like to root for the underdog.

Everyone knows what a landscaper does. But many of our roles and businesses are more esoteric and technical. If people struggle to get who you are and what you do, try creating a side-by-side.

By drawing contrasts and comparisons, you help answer the unspoken (or verbalized) questions quickly and memorably.

CHAPTER 14:

Summaries

"Perhaps the best test of a man's intelligence is his capacity for making a summary."
—LYTTON STRACHEY

Earlier, I discussed how one of the active verbs in communication design is "solidify." A summary is one of the best ways to nail down understanding and agreement. Brief recaps (or previews) are far easier for the human brain to process and remember than long-form explanations.

A summary is a brief overview or condensed version of a longer text, speech, or other piece of content. It provides a concise condensation of the most important information or ideas, while omitting less relevant details or examples.

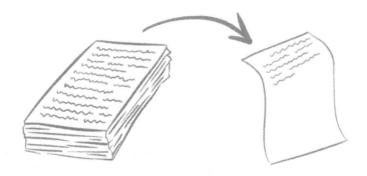

The purpose of a summary is to provide a reader with a quick understanding of the main points of the original work, without having to read the entire thing. You can use summaries for a variety of purposes, such as:

- Studying or reviewing material for a test or exam.
- Providing an overview of a complex topic to someone who is not familiar with it.
- Briefing colleagues or team members on a report or presentation.
- Sharing the key takeaways of a book or article with others.

Details are for being comprehensive. Summaries are for the quick scan.

Details are for being comprehensive. Summaries are for the quick scan.

When we read or listen to information, our brains process it in short-term memory. However, if we want to transfer that information to long-term memory, we need to actively engage with it and make connections between the new information and our existing knowledge. Summarizing information helps us do this by forcing us to focus on the key points and concepts, which in turn helps us remember them more easily. Additionally, summaries often use simple language and clear organization, making them easier to understand and remember.

In organizations, most high-level summary statements (purpose, vision, mission, values) are poorly composed and unmemorable. Generic summaries are ineffective, but the concept of a distilled statement of core ideas is valuable, if it is well crafted. No one is going to memorize a detailed thirty-page handbook.

Churches often have confessions of faith, key doctrine overviews, and catechisms. Each of these summaries is a shortcut to turning the light on in the minds of the faithful and is foundational to agreement and alignment.

Recently, I was doing a clarity workshop with a corporate customer (with its Learning and Development department), and it became clear that there was a disconnect between what one member of the team considered her job role to be and what others were assuming. Nothing malicious was involved; there was a misunderstanding because they were not all aligned around a simple (written) summary of her prime responsibilities and activities.

Another area where this shows up constantly is with meetings. The best meetings have a clear up-front summary (agenda) and a simple and brief post-meeting summary that outlines the results of the meeting and any action items pending. If things are left floating in the air without solidification, there is no hope for gaining alignment.

The table of contents and introduction of this book are forms of summary. You want to have a 30,000-foot view of what you're getting in a few minutes before trying to digest the entire book.

To summarize, here's why you want to generously use summaries:

- They're quick to scan.
- They're easy to process.
- They make entry into memory more likely.
- They show respect for the audience's time and bandwidth.

Now, to summarize this section of the book: By judiciously employing the tools outlined above, you make it much easier for your audience to grasp your intentions and understand the point. Shortcuts are the brain-friendly way to quickly turn on the light and activate the memory.

They also make your message a whole lot more fun to receive. Why be boring when you can spark interest and engagement with stories, symbols, snippets, and other tools?

If what you're communicating is important, make it sticky. Chip and Dan Heath,[34] using an analogy to Velcro, put it this way in the book *Made To Stick*: "Your brain hosts a truly staggering number of loops. The more hooks an idea has, the better it will cling to memory."

If you're like me, you want to get your message across and embedded as fast as possible. Now you know how. It's time to put all these principles and practices to work.

Part 4:

Applying Clarity Best Practices

Most of us communicate in a variety of ways—writing, speaking, leading, coaching, interviewing, and so on. The Clarity Fuel Formula applies to all these modalities because the human brain wants what it wants the way it wants it, no matter what means of communication we're using.

Think about your most memorable teachers, trainers, and leaders. One thing they probably all had in common is this: You understood what they were saying. They made sure of it.

You may be a CEO, or you may be a new hire. You may be shy, or you may be bold. Young or old, famous or obscure, you can be great at communicating with clarity.

In my client workshops, we typically focus on a specific group (emerging leaders, field managers, sales representatives, technical specialists, key company leaders, or the like) and then address one or more particular communication practices (for example, marketing, presentation skills, email skills, professional/personal branding, or coaching skills). The clarity principles are universal, but the training/upskilling applications are many and specific.

Let's dive into some practical ways you can immediately become more effective by redesigning ten formats of communication: email, presentations, teaching and training, leadership, collaboration, purpose statements, branding, personal branding and career direction, social media, and networking. And for each communication method, remember: You can gain sharper focus by applying the A-to-B Shift exercise.

CHAPTER 15:

Email

*"To be an effective communicator,
it's important to ensure that your emails are clear,
direct, and correctly understood."*

—RYAN FOLAND

The death of email has long been prophesied, but as with the end of the world, the predictions just keep missing the mark. As of 2022, we are sending 333.2 billion emails per day[35] around the globe. That volume of electronic messages represents an enormous number of potential opportunities gained—or lost.

Email is not a bad thing. But bad emails are definitely a thing. That's why we have a Delete key. I was about to guess that the most quickly worn-out selection on a keyboard is the Delete key, but Google informs me that it's the space bar. Dang. That would have made a great snippet.

Composing punchy, effective emails is your best training for putting clarity into practice. Each day, multiple times a day, you can apply all the tactics you've learned in this book. When you and your team master email clarity, the rest will come naturally.

> **Composing punchy, effective emails is your best training for putting clarity into practice.**

You know what they say about first impressions? Well, with email, you only have a moment to gain the eye contact and attention of your inbox-skimming reader. Real-tors talk about the visual influence of curb appeal. Our email messages need content appeal.

So, be sure to take full advantage of the most import-ant visual real estate of your message, which is the subject line and the first sentence. Set a hook to draw the recipient in, then make the rest of the message easy to absorb.

How can your email design become more brain-friendly and effective? Here are some simple suggestions.

- Why are you sending this message? What's the intended result? Have a clear Point B before you start composing.

- Make it obvious up-front what matters most about this message and what the recipient should do about it. Bring the call to action (perhaps with a deadline) forward into the subject line or first paragraph.

- Nearly half of emails are now read on mobile devices, and that gives us a very small piece of visual real estate. Be brief and direct, or you'll lose attention and engagement by demanding too much effort (and scrolling) to figure out message relevance. Mobile-friendly is brain-friendly.

- Inside the main text of the message, consider judi-ciously using a highlight or a bold font for the main point to ensure that the busy reader immedi-ately grasps the purpose.

- Use white space to avoid a jumbled overload of words. Keep paragraphs short and use line breaks to make it easier for the eye to scan.
- Whenever possible, compose brief, single-focus messages that a reader can respond to immediately, instead of trying to cover multiple themes. If you require your recipients to engage in too much thought about multiple topics, you are less likely to generate a quick response and may create unintended confusion.
- If your communication needs to be longer or more complex, use bullet points to provide quick, easy-to-skim summaries. Use a link or an attachment to address details, instead of overloading the message. Stratify your information.
- If you're engaged in an email chain of forwarded messages, consider limiting the number of copied recipients, or summarize the content, or perhaps even change the subject line to something more relevant. Long chains of loosely connected messages are inherently confusing—they're too much work to process.

Axios commissioned Gallup to do a poll on work communications.[36] One of the findings was that 70 percent of employees want shorter digital communications at work (only 4 percent wanted longer items). Furthermore, only 20 percent strongly agreed that their leaders communicate effectively with the rest of the organization. That's a lot of room for improvement.

Millions of emails—many of them very important—are dead on inbox arrival because of brain-unfriendly communication design. There's no obvious up-front relevance. If every single person and company was trained to follow these simple email clarity practices, the return on investment (ROI) would be incalculable.

CHAPTER 16:

Presentations

"Words that are carefully framed and spoken are the most powerful means of communication there is."

—NANCY DUARTE

I love designing and giving presentations. Like every other speaker, I've had some winners and some snoozers. Phillip Khan-Panni, UK champion business speaker and author, estimates that 80 percent of presentations fail to deliver on their objective.[37] Ouch.

There's a tremendous opportunity to step into the premier 20 percent level by applying a handful of simple practices, one of which is having a clear road map toward a desirable end point.

According to Eva Daniel at The Speak Shop, it is vital to let your audience know right away where you are taking them in the talk—or they won't go with you. You should tuck between an opening and the main body of the presentation a brief preview road map that sketches out the destination and the promise of the talk. I've recently begun opening my workshops with very tangible "end result" promises such as, "the very next email you send after our time together will be noticeably better—guaranteed."

I asked Eva what specific benefits a typical audience member might walk away with as a result of her presentation about great public speaking. It's easy to put forward a generic statement such as, "you'll be a better speaker," but that isn't sticky and motivating. Eva points to three tangible WIIFM results she expects to bring about:

- Audience members who apply her principles will save a bunch of time in preparation.
- Skillfully crafted and presented talks will help establish you as a thought leader.
- Skillful speakers will create far better audience engagement during a presentation.

The opposite of this advice is data-dumping. In the pharmaceutical industry, there is a notorious tendency for "thought leaders" and others to display information-dense slides and just read off of them. That's not communication; it's narration. If you have to convey dense or complex information, the best way to approach the presentation is to extract a main point for the slide and emphasize it verbally with some sort of brief illustrative or explanatory introduction. Give the audience a quick summary or highlight up-front to increase engagement.

Your audience is silently begging for a reason to tune in and focus. Their RAS is looking for a WIIFM. So, when presenting to a live or online audience, have a clear up-front hook—a distinct statement of purpose or a striking snippet—to secure engagement. Then create a simple, logical flow that leads to a clear destination.

- The unspoken question on the minds of everyone in your audience is, "Why?" Answer that in the first minute and avoid prefacing the main body of the presentation with loads of background, history, and discussion of process. Nobody cares about that right off. Tell people what you've got and where you're taking them, not how you got there.

- Avoid the temptation to overload your audience's brains with TMI. Information density—too much data and visual busyness for the brain to process—is the killer of many presentations. As you plan your material, think about this: What are the one or two things I *really* want people to walk away with? Then prune the excess.

- If you're presenting in front of a group, your value-add is as a guide and commentator, not as a slide-narrator or data-dispenser. Present a compact theme or message on each slide, accompanied by no more than one graphic. Simple, immediate absorption is the goal. If there is a deeper set of data and details, you can cover these in the verbal description, handouts, or follow-up slides designed for conveying denser content.

- Use a much simpler design approach than you might for a set of slides designed for in-depth documentation. Marketing guru Guy Kawasaki advocated the 10-20-30 Rule:[38] slide presentations should have at most 10 slides, last no more than 20 minutes, and contain no font smaller than 30 points. Some types of presentations cannot be reduced to this extent, but it's a great exercise when developing your slides to use a framework like this for maintaining clarity and simplicity.

- Weave in stories to secure emotional engagement. Sprinkle in some humor and personal anecdotes. Give tangible examples to illustrate specific points. Play a video clip. Include visual snippets. The brain cannot concentrate with unrelenting intensity, so create a cadence of lighter moments as you build your presentation flow.
- Never use tiny labels, overly detailed visuals/graphics, or low-contrast text and background color combinations. A squinting and confused listener is going to be frustrated and unable to absorb the message.

When presenting to a live or online audience, have a clear up-front hook to secure engagement.

Here's a bonus tip: If you have friends or colleagues who are thoughtful and reasonably articulate, you may want to review the first draft of your presentation with them (video calls are great for this). You are often too close to your own material, and it can be very helpful to see how someone from the outside is reacting to your content flow and design.

Michael Stelzner, author and public speaking pro, has spent many hours evaluating good communication skills in his role as founder and CEO of Social Media Examiner and the Social Media Marketing World conference.[39] One of his approaches to creating audience engagement is to go beyond incidental storytelling, to immersing the listeners in the flow of a real-life meta-narrative. For instance, he might begin the journey with a provocative claim or challenge, mention events and memes from recent history, and then show where trends are really heading, wrapping it all up with a moral to the story. This combination of familiarity and insight is a powerful technique to keep an audience engaged.

There's a hidden price tag to delivering a talk that fails to deliver the goods. If eighty businesspeople spend one hour disengaging from an ineffective presentation, that's two expensive work weeks (eighty hours, in aggregate) of unrecoverable time. Then add the future opportunity costs of not moving the audience toward insight and action. It's well worth the investment of time to make sure that every presentation has a brain-friendly design.

You're not being asked merely to deliver a presentation. You're being asked to deliver value. What will your audience walk away with that will spark discussion, insight, and change?

CHAPTER 17:

Teaching and Training

*"Where my reason, imagination or interest were not
engaged, I would not or I could not learn."*
—WINSTON CHURCHILL

If you're in a classroom (physical or virtual), you probably have a captive audience for some period of time. But while their bodies may be present, their minds can be far away. The best thing you can do for your captives is to be consistently captivating.

For short messages (a thirty-second ad, an email, a quick social media video), you need to capture attention once, at the start. But for longer formats, like a class, you must continually recapture and renew attention with brain-engaging shortcuts and other interesting tactics.

Great teachers and trainers make ideas come alive. They don't just transmit, they illuminate. Some of my best professors in college used props. I still remember one physics professor who dragged in an actual bed of nails and laid down on it. I don't know how he got permission to store that monstrosity year after year, but he sure made his point (pun intended)!

I have often used a couple of stuffed animals (a pigeon, to explain why pigeonholing is important to your brand; and a penguin, as an example of a creature that blends into the crowd). Unlike the bed of nails, these props are easy to throw around. They would, however, seem a bit weird in a carry-on, so I put them in checked luggage.

Whatever tools you use to grab audience attention, ultimately, the flow of the material has to be brain-friendly. Unstructured information leaves it to the listener to sort through the haystack and find the needle. Teachers and trainers are there to prioritize and make sense of the information. Start with simplicity.

> **Unstructured information leaves it to the listener to sort through the haystack and find the needle. Teachers and trainers are there to prioritize and make sense of the information.**

As marketing consultant Tom Martin once put it[40] when coaching a coworker to be clearer and more specific in a presentation, "this makes no sense to anyone who isn't you." The Curse of Knowledge leads you to leave out important information when you're at the front of the room because you assume that your audience already knows what you know. The safest bet is to assume the opposite.

If you're teaching or training, you're in a great position to employ the rules and the tools I've discussed earlier in this book.

- Map out your content into major points, minor points, and supporting information. Stratify. Not everything is of equal importance, weight, or relevance. Answer these questions in preparation: What matters most? Why does it matter? How should I expect my audience to respond and act?
- Let learners know the relevance and the stakes right away. In Malcolm Knowles's, PhD, six assump-

tions of Adult Learning, the first one is explaining the "why" for the lesson.

- Generously weave illustrative and interesting stories into every lesson. Bare principles and facts can dampen attention. Stories make your message come to life.

- Some part of your role when in front of a group is, dare I say it, to entertain. You're not only there to impart gems of wisdom, but to make the process enjoyable. One of my favorite techniques is to do a dramatic reading of a passage of incomprehensible jargon in my best radio-narrator voice. It always creates a laugh—and makes the point in definite and memorable fashion.

- Use the news. Current events are on everybody's mind. If you can tie a specific principle to yesterday's headline, you have a shortcut into the attention and emotions of your audience.

- Ask audience members to provide their own instances about how a particular principle or theme worked itself out in their lives. Pull stories from them, and riff on those narratives.

- Remember that a captive audience will resent tedious information transactions. Bored students are the fault of the presenter. If you've never seen Robin Williams as the engaging teacher in the movie *Dead Poets Society*, I recommend you watch it immediately. You'll never forget his summary of a dry and dreary poetry textbook as "excrement!"

Not every member of an audience responds the same way to each kind of content. Michael Stelzner advocates for presenting ideas using a variety of means: for example, stories, data, or graphics. Every communicator knows that human beings hear selectively, and forget quickly, so bringing back a previously mentioned nugget or attaching a new story to an important point helps ensure that the point is getting across. That's solidifying.

Gaining attention up-front is crucial; maintaining engagement through exercises and interaction is when real learning occurs. David Davis, president of Romar Learning Solutions and corporate trainer extraordinaire, summarizes the golden rule his wife Wanda (also an educator) uses regularly:[41] "Whoever is doing the work is doing the learning." If the instructor is doing all the work by droning on and on without creating regular practical application of the principles and practices by students, the learners lose interest. Illumination and involvement work hand-in-hand.

As you look at the whole sweep and flow of your content, keep asking the questions: How can I turn the light on here? How can I illustrate this? How can I make this relevant? How can I make this a more engaging experience? Your audience will thank you for the effort.

CHAPTER 18:

Leadership

*"90% of all management problems
are caused by miscommunication"*
—DALE CARNEGIE

When I was in medical device sales, I shared responsibility for business development with a colleague. I had one half of the US and Canada; my colleague had the other half. However, I had one skill set, while my colleague had different strengths. We were both frustrated with half of our roles.

A new manager saw the struggles we were having and had a moment of leadership clarity. He suggested that we split responsibilities not by geography, but by competency (new customer acquisition/marketing for me, customer/technical support for my coworker). That made a dramatic difference and set us both up for success.

This was the first dawning of a vital realization that later came to fuller expression when I read the book *Now, Discover Your Strengths.*[42] Leadership involves talent management. And talent management means proactively wrapping words around unique personal or professional characteristics and putting people in the right roles. Clarity of identity and purpose is a precursor to clarity of expectations.

Leaders also provide clarity of message. They do not rely on magic or mind reading to align their teams and move them forward. It comes down to clear and actionable ideas expressed in clear words: being proactive, not hands-off, vague, or indecisive. Setting people up for success takes human intelligence, not the artificial kind.

Leaders need to set the direction and communicate the direction—unambiguously.

> **Leaders need to set the direction and communicate the direction— unambiguously.**

Effective leaders are regularly answering these (spoken or unspoken) questions with simple, brief statements:

- What are our goals and direction as a team/organization? (Destination)
- What does good look like? (Definition)
- What is the next step? (Decision-making)
- What are my responsibilities, overall and day to day? (Delegation)

How can effective leaders employ clarity principles and practices on a day-to-day level?

- Make it one of your top goals to help every team member gain self-awareness by identifying their value and their strengths. Help them arrive at the keywords that summarize their professional identity. This practice is key to cultivating talent and creating productive long-term engagement.
- If employees are unclear about their day-to-day responsibilities, ask them what they perceive to be their three main priorities, in 1-2-3 order, and

then explain and clarify what you are expecting until you achieve understanding and alignment.

- Practice imparting clear details and tangibles. Goals, priorities, processes, outcomes, deliverables—all should be as practical and measurable as possible. While visionary people can thrive with various levels of ambiguity and creativity (that's why we have entrepreneurs), most people prefer a far more defined set of specifics to work within. Ambiguity does not set people up for success.

- Praise team members by pointing out very specific contributions. Not just, "Good job on the Acme account" but "Your follow-up skills with Acme over the past three months really set a great example for everyone in the company to follow."

- Consider creating specific purpose statements for each part of the organization. For example, the practical goals of the HR department are different from those of the sales team, which are quite different from the IT group. "Branding" each group creates a clearer identity, culture, and set of expectations. Every team has a different What, For Whom, Why, How, and Where.

- Assemble stories that sum up the values and successes of the organization and disseminate them regularly. Stories will inform and inspire more readily than bare principles.

Some of these practices will take on different shapes in larger organizations. Jennifer Muszik,[43] who has led learning teams for field-based colleagues in multinational companies like Pfizer, Roche, and Biogen, says that one important element of achieving the buy-in of global stakeholders is to focus on gaining clarity at the highest strategic level. Aligning on big-picture intention is more important than fixating on tactical details, which will often vary considerably from country to country. Collaboration and "getting on the same page" in this case means majoring on the overall direction and minoring on the specific directives.

When I asked my friend John Novello,[44] a noted jazz musician, about how he practices clarity with other musicians during a live performance, he emphasized majoring on the overall direction and minoring on the specific directives. Because jazz music is strongly improvisational, getting on the same page is more situational and dynamic than, say, conducting an orchestra with a precise and fixed score.

In the corporate training world, content developers are often encouraged to come up with "learning objectives" for a class, workshop, or course. But such statements are often quite generic, even ambiguous, says Jeffrey Taylor,[45] who has decades of experience training pharmaceutical sales representatives and leaders. Instead, you should craft skill-based performance objectives that employees can easily observe on the job. These are practical expectations based on specific behavior and attitude changes.

Training design is all about moving from one state of performance to a better one, not merely imparting knowledge. Every leader, manager, and trainer should become proficient at articulating on-the-job expectations that are well defined to set people up for success and create a healthy culture of accountability.

Leaders, managers, and coaches are in a unique position to help build a focused culture of engaged employees. This occurs best when VUCA is counteracted by a steady diet of clarity.

CLARITY SPOTLIGHT

Steve Haase, leadership coach at Superabound Coaching,[46] underscored the need to set clear expectations for job roles by describing his long-ago audition to play trumpet in the US Navy band.

His talent won him an offer, but this was not a position with a vague and lofty job description. He and his colleagues would be shivering outside in snow and rain or sweating in uniform while retiring officers recounted one too many tales from their previous glory days.

The leader of the interview was not pulling any wool over his eyes. Candidates were plainly warned that this job was not in some cushy symphony hall gig; the New York Philharmonic might be in the future, but for now, it would be lots of grunt, little glory. Was he OK with that?

He was. The expectations were clear. He knew exactly what he and his trumpet were walking into.

CHAPTER 19:

Collaboration

"Collaboration is a key part of the success of any organization, executed through a clearly defined vision and mission and based on transparency and constant communication."

—DINESH PALIWAL

Few of us work alone. Tom Hanks, trapped alone on a South Pacific island in the movie *Cast Away*, only had a volleyball ("Wilson") to interact with, but the rest of us are surrounded by pesky humans with all their crazy ideas, personal foibles, and different understandings.

In other words, we must collaborate. And the many Wilsons in our lives have brains and hearts very different from our own.

Quarrel over the words up-front instead of fighting over the results later. Get on the same page early so you don't end up on opposite teams later.

Unified effort can only come from aligned expectations. You must provide a clear (written) map to the destination, and the process for getting there. Begin with the end in mind and then reverse-engineer the steps to get there. Here are some tips:

- Don't expect multiple stakeholders to magically have common goals, expectations, and mental metadata around any initiative. Instead, articulate the highest-level goal (the peak of the stratification pyramid) and gain verbal and written agreement on that before moving to a deeper outline of expectations and processes (middle of the pyramid). Only then can you progress to alignment on the details (base of the pyramid).

- Practice iterative development on your projects. Start with the simplest framework and gain agreement, then move to the next level of development. Continue stepwise so that refinement and alignment progressively improve. Don't expect any project to move forward correctly without frequent check-ins and checkups.

- A written plan, both at the high level and the detailed level, is the key to successful collaboration. You can only achieve correct action and accountability with written expectations. Verbal agreements inevitably lead to misunderstandings.

- When working with external vendors, be sure to schedule a kickoff meeting where everyone gets to agree on all expectations, timelines, and variables. It's vital at the start of any project to get key internal and external stakeholders to agree on process and deliverables.

- Define and assign specific responsibilities. Every stakeholder should be clear about their contribution (and their boundaries). Whenever possible, have one designated project manager who is responsible for timelines, reviews/approvals, and communications. If multiple cooks are making the broth, and input is scattered, chaos is inevitable.

- Write out a clear purpose and agenda for each meeting and provide written summaries afterward to ensure agreement and alignment.

Unified effort can only come from aligned expectations.

Simplicity and brevity are crucial to clear communications, but in certain instances, so is detailed completeness. Every consultant or vendor has encountered clients that are foggy about what they want. Proactively pose purposeful, focused questions to dig beneath the surface to get to the true need and goal. This will replace vagueness with clarity and is one of the greatest values you can add to your work environment.

Learning consultant Kim Catania described a large-scale project for a client that wanted to update all home-study and onboarding materials for new hires. The mandate the client originally gave was too broad and general to execute on—there was no well-articulated destination or timeline. But once extensive interviews, detailed analysis, curriculum mapping, and design development took place, it became a million-dollar project. Achieving such rich clarity was so successful, and the client was so pleased with the result, that eventually the growing client company became a multimillion-dollar account.

Many companies work with a "matrixed" organization, with dotted lines of responsibility, and a high need to collaborate broadly to reach consensus and move forward. When bringing together people from multiple disciplines, it is even more vital to use simple and straightforward language to ensure shared meaning.

Since many professionals in our global economy interact regularly with people who are not native English speakers, it is critical to use the simplest and plainest terminology. Jack Appleman tells his clients to write as they speak; if they're struggling with how to write up a report or proposal, he asks them, "What are you trying to say? Verbalize it."

I recently employed a similar technique with a business leader who was struggling to compose a useful set of purpose statements for an operations group at a major media company. The first draft was far too abstract, so I simply asked, "Well, what are these people *doing*? What is their hands-on purpose and value in the organization?" The next attempted answer was still vague, so I asked the same questions again. That's when the right words began to tumble out.

Define, summarize, and document. That's how you get collaborators on the same page.

CHAPTER 20:

Purpose Statements

"The most effective way I know to begin with the end in mind is to develop a personal mission statement or philosophy or creed. It focused on what you want to be (character) and to do (contributions and achievements) and on the values or principles upon which being and doing are based."

—STEPHEN COVEY

S imon Sinek made the following phrase famous: "Start with why." He even wrote an excellent book with that title.[47]

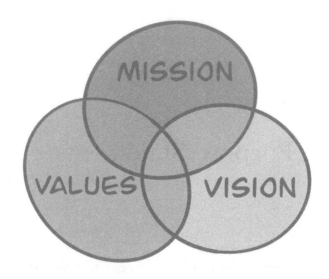

We practical-minded humans are often obsessed with the What. That's important, but the What doesn't have meaning or purpose without the Why. That's the fuel that drives people forward. It's the foundation of organizational culture. And a clear Why always makes it much easier to arrive at a correct What and How.

Positioning and purpose statements provide the north star for any company, large or small, to express exactly why they exist. They are the foundation stones of a brand. They are powerful for shaping culture and for informing day-to-day decisions. Clear statements help create aligned teams—and even keep individuals on track.

Unless they are horribly generic and vague, like this entry from Edward Jones:

"At Edward Jones, our purpose is to partner for positive impact to improve the lives of our clients and colleagues, and together, better our communities and society."[48]

Wait, what? That could apply to any sort of company on earth! That's not a clear or differentiating purpose, that's a greeting card.

"_____ is an organization with one clear purpose: to make a difference in people's lives. Our employees are an important part of it all." Two generic statements in one purpose! Out of 259,000 possibilities, what kind of organization do you think this is? (Nope, wrong guess. It's M&T Bank).[49]

Harley-Davidson didn't set out just to create a motorcycle. Anyone can cobble together a motorbike. It created a community. A cult, if you will. "We create products, services and experiences that inspire our customers to discover adventure, find freedom for the soul and live the Harley-Davidson lifestyle."[50]

A great example of a purpose statement is the one for charity: water. "charity: water is a nonprofit organization bringing clean and safe water to people around the world." The summary is plain: "Since charity: water was founded in 2006, we've been chasing one ambitious goal: ending the global water crisis. And while the water crisis is huge, we're optimistic. We know how to solve the problem, and we make progress every day thanks to the help of local partners and generous supporters."[51]

The reader knows exactly what the intent is; there's a specific focus with a clear result.

But then there is this kind of generic, windy statement: "Our purpose is to create a better everyday for everyone to build a better life for all." What does that even mean?

While it sounds like another nonprofit, in fact, this is from global services giant Sodexo, which also describes itself on its website thusly: "we promote quality of life at work through customized solutions that help businesses, public institutions, managers of prestigious venues and organizers of major events to create welcoming, creative, effective and innovative solutions, for all."[52]

I'm very confused.

When it comes to employees, a sense of purpose is what drives people to do more than the bare minimum. Purpose statements should be brief, practical, and specific to create clarity and motivation.

- If you're an organizational executive, don't settle for vague, generic purpose statements that could apply to a thousand other companies. Nobody will remember and enthusiastically embrace such me-too principles. "We practice Innovation, Customer-Centricity, and Excellence"—blah. "Our Values are Integrity, Caring, and Diversity"—just like everyone else. "We exist to advance human flourishing by providing products that elevate well-being"—how original!

- Be focused. No business can be all things to all people. You can't plug three destinations into your GPS. An effective purpose statement is a pair of corrective lenses, designed to provide 20/20 vision of exactly where you're heading. For a massive company (100 brands in 100 countries), General

Mills has a very simple purpose at its foundation: "We make food the world loves."

- Aim for something authentically aspirational. A purpose implies something helpful, something higher, something better. "We exist to provide average, midrange products that no one cares about" is not going to attract talent, investment, or customers. How *specifically* do you plan to make a difference in the lives of people? What is that difference (the A-to-B Shift writ large).

- Eliminate every whiff of jargon. No "leverage." No "scalable end-to-end platforms." No "game-changing mission-critical synergy." You're going to sit down with your third-grade teacher and explain what your company does. Use third-grade language.

- One high-level set of purpose statements may not be adequate for all the divisions and departments of a larger organization. Each division has its own specific purpose, and people in those departments need to align with their unique organizational value. Targeted purpose statements make it much easier to determine strategic direction for those groups (and to make correct hires).

Let's head back to some of my local coffee shops. All my local favorites are reasonably good places to meet with people for business purposes, and they all serve good coffee and treats. Most of them, however, feel a little claustrophobic. A bit crowded and rushed.

But one of them also has a clear purpose of creating a comfortable community setting for young mothers/families to meet in. How do I know this? It's roomy. There are two spacious play areas with toys and rugs. Stuffed animals on the shelves. A big table with eight chairs for group meetings. Moms and kids love the place. (Also— great sausage rolls!) The owner sums up the environment they are creating with three words: authentic, spacious, and welcoming.

In fact, as I am writing this paragraph, a dad talks to his friend and plays Connect Four with his three-year-old. That wouldn't happen at Starbucks. All those young parents are spending money, Instagramming their experience, and roping in their other friends, who are also enjoying the space and spending money. Why? Purposeful design that fulfills the stated intent. Sometimes design is just as eloquent as words when conveying purpose.

Seek to distill *the* differentiating value you are bringing to your marketplace in one brief sentence. What is my primary purpose as the King of Clarity? To teach people how to become great communicators using the Clarity Fuel Formula. That simple phrase keeps me on target.

Once you know your clear "Yes!", you can much more readily say "No!" to the rest.

> **Once you know your clear "Yes!", you can much more readily say "No!" to the rest.**

Actually, Simon Sinek, at the beginning of his afore-mentioned book, has a very simple and vivid purpose statement: "Simon Sinek is leading a movement to inspire people to do what inspires them." Clean, brief, focused, and memorable.

It's easy to articulate small-ball goals; to grow to x level, to be more profitable, to take over the world in the next decade. Well, maybe that last bit isn't small-ball. But what is your "leave things much better than how I found them" big-picture purpose? Can you share that, in one sentence, with your family and friends? That's what will give clarity for all of your other decisions in life and business.

CLARITY SPOTLIGHT

Branding a department with purpose: What's that all about?

Jason Zeman had a challenge in front of him—one which drew on all his skills as builder of systems, curricula, and people.

He took over a training department in a rapidly growing company. There had been so much change that the department had no real identity—as with training departments in many organizations, they were viewed as doers, not strategic partners. The group not only needed a message; it needed purpose statements.

Jason knew how vital clarity had been to his own professional identity, so he organized a hands-on workshop to articulate a clear purpose for the team, including keywords, statements, and stories that would shape the perception of the rest of the organization—and provide a foundation for culture and focused action.[53]

The initiative was so successful that the department was soon given additional responsibilities and more staffing. The departmental branding approach spread to global HR and leadership development in the coming years, which also led to communications and personal branding workshops for annual cohorts of emerging leaders.

CHAPTER 21:

Branding

"Products are made in the factory,
but brands are created in the mind."
—WALTER LANDOR

The goal of branding is to occupy mind-space and heart-trust. You've succeeded in building an awesome brand when you are top of mind (memory) and tip of tongue (referrals).

Quick question: Which car company has managed to own the keyword/snippet "safety" over the decades? Right—Volvo. That one core concept is central to its brand.

I once worked for a company with a forgettable name, but a memorable product. Whenever we'd talk to potential clients, a look of puzzlement would cross their face when we mentioned the company name. But as soon as we used the name of the online learning software platform we'd created, their eyes would light up: "Oh, you're the Pedagogue people!"

As it turns out, we were doing other types of custom software work—but the marketplace had already settled on our most distinctive core identity and offering. We already owned a piece of memory real estate. People, all of whom have limited brain bandwidth, like to remember companies for one or two things, not for a bunch of random stuff.

Since we already had some kind of brand recognition—a label people recognized—we did the only logical thing. We changed the name of the company to mirror the name of the product.

You've succeeded in building an awesome brand when you are top of mind (memory) and tip of tongue (referrals).

Most people think of names, logos, and taglines as the essence of the brand, but that's only part of the story—that's the surface and outward expression. Others point out that your brand is the experience people have of you in the marketplace—their perceptions. That is true, but when it comes to a clear outward-facing message, the real foundation of the brand can be found in the statements and stories that sum up your specialness. Branding is idea and message encapsulation using words that get the point across.

In other words, clarity in branding is accurately articulating your unique value and your niche (your marketplace sweet spot), in brief and memorable words and images. You're going to pigeonhole yourself, because riches are in the niches.

- Center your message on the main pain you're relieving or hope you're fulfilling for your audience (their WIIFM). Your target customer is looking for help and results, not platitudes.
- Define your niche and your unique value proposition. Don't settle for a generic message that sounds like a hundred other companies and fails to set you apart in the mind of the listener. Commodity providers are not memorable.

- Find an interesting angle that appeals to the RAS. If you're not outstanding and somehow remarkable, then you're forgettable. You never want to be just another banker/realtor/consultant/digital marketing firm. Read Seth Godin's classic marketing book *Purple Cow* for a great explanation of this idea.

- Your brand should be summarized in five clear statements: **What** (exactly what solution/product you are providing); **for Whom** (your specific target customer); **Why** (the customer pain or aspiration you're addressing); **How** (your unique superpower/capabilities); and **Where** (the geographic or marketplace areas you serve). Such well-crafted statements are the compass for marketing direction, sales efforts, and strategic decision-making.

- Make your brand offering/message tangible and easy to describe (particularly for someone who might want to refer you). Tell stories that paint the picture. Use symbolic language that will leverage a memory hook. Are you the Mercedes-Benz of your category? Own it and use the analogy.

I encourage my clients who are seeking to create punchy brand statements to craft a short-form sound bite like this:

"We provide (this specific offering) to (this very specific target market—what I call the 'bullseye customer') in order to (fix this pain/meet this pressing need) through our (differentiating superpower)."

For example:

"CARE Service is a personalized transportation service that helps people with physical limitations in the tristate area travel safely to and from their healthcare and other appointments. Not just a curb-to-curb car service—door-to-door CARE service."

A brief, vivid summary of your unique value to the marketplace is key to your branding efforts. Brand messaging is the verbal shorthand that allows others to accurately remember and refer you.

My *Clarity Wins*[54] book explains these branding and referral concepts in much more detail.

CLARITY SPOTLIGHT

Romar Learning Solutions served its clientele successfully for years before it became obvious that it hadn't differentiated itself from other training providers in the life sciences space. Clients often came back for more development work, but the projects had such variety that it was challenging to find an overarching theme.

The company knew it was good, and so did its clients. But the marketplace was noisy and so many of the messages going out from the vendors sounded like carbon copies of each other.

We conducted a facilitated group session with the Romar team to outline its top successes, determine its key strengths, and find a way to clearly communicate its areas of expertise in a way that stood out from other providers. It suffered from a common malady in the marketplace—it did a lot of things that seemed disconnected from each other.

Narrowing the company's many capabilities into a single core message was daunting, but we were able to reach consensus and distill it down to a clearly stated identity that tied together its whole body of work. One of the key elements was to create a message that was specific, yet broad enough that it could continue to grow into the message as the company continued to evolve in coming years.

The Romar team then relaunched its website and updated its marketing materials to communicate a single, prominent message that clearly communicates the company's expertise and puts forth what makes it unique in the learning industry.[55]

CHAPTER 22:

Personal Branding and Career Direction

"All of us need to understand the importance of branding. We are CEOs of our own companies: Me Inc. To be in business today, our most important job is to be head marketer for the brand called You."

—TOM PETERS

What you're about to read is a real, live overview on LinkedIn of someone's current role:

"Leading cross-functional commercial operations teams in building sustainable capabilities across a large global matrix organization focused on co-creating, evolving and implementing integrated and efficient Multichannel, Marketing Excellence and Sales Excellence processes across Regions, and Countries by innovating and continuously improving frameworks, tools, and platforms driven by business insights, engagement with Region and Affiliate partners, analyzing and benchmarking capabilities, in and outside the industry, and delivering best-in-class capabilities that drive superior performance."

Um…who are you and what do you do, exactly? That's generic commodity language. Obscure jargon. Definitely not remarkable, nor memorable. Nor brief.

Marketing expert Mark Schaefer put it this way in his book, *The Content Code*: "The key to finding your remarkability is to think about what makes you surprising, interesting, or novel."[56] Ability $\Rightarrow$ Remarkability $\Rightarrow$ Marketability.

Mark wrote the book *KNOWN* with the conviction that, increasingly, the personal brand is our only sustainable competitive advantage. When you know who you are and what you do well, and can express that clearly to others, you build human bridges that ads and algorithms cannot replicate.

In a world increasingly dominated by automation and artificial intelligence, the trusted professional who can bring insight, creativity, and practical application will become more important every year. Information is a commodity. Hard-earned trusted expertise is a scarce and valuable resource.

What is personal branding? Essentially, it's the way people perceive you, your reputation, and what you represent. It can influence the opportunities you attract, the relationships you build, and your overall success. Here are some specific reasons why a personal brand is important:

1. **Differentiation:** In a competitive job market or business world, having a strong personal brand can help you differentiate yourself from others. It allows you to highlight your unique strengths, skills, and experiences, which can make you more attractive to potential employers, clients, or collaborators.

2. **Credibility:** A strong personal brand can help establish your credibility and expertise in your field. It can demonstrate your knowledge, skills, and experience, which can increase people's trust and confidence in you.

3. **Networking:** Your personal brand can also help you expand your network and connect with like-minded individuals or potential clients or collaborators. It can facilitate meaningful conversations

and interactions, which can lead to new opportunities or partnerships.

4. **Career advancement:** A strong personal brand can help you advance your career and achieve your professional goals. It can increase your visibility and reputation in your field, which can lead to new job offers or promotions.

5. **Consistency:** Developing a personal brand requires you to be intentional and consistent in your actions, communication, and behaviors. This can help you develop good habits, increase your self-awareness, and build a strong reputation over time.

Some people find the idea of personal branding to have an "icky" factor, as if it's hollow self-promotion, but that's not the point. It's simply a summary of your identity and value to the marketplace. Personal branding is YOU effectively projected in words that work.

Personal branding is YOU effectively projected in words that work.

People are going to think thoughts of you. Why not shape those ideas with accurate words instead of leaving it to chance?

Self-awareness, with strengths and value summarized in keywords and brief phrases, will be your guide to making the best career decisions. What differentiates you? What do people say about your strengths?

Your personal brand is intimately tied to your career direction. Here's some advice about being self-aware as you navigate your career:

- Don't seek a new role without considering whether you are actually a good fit for that job and whether that job is a good fit for your goals. Some promotions or advancements can be bad opportunities—for you. Instead, develop your own personal/professional value statements (and keywords and stories) that will serve as your personal GPS when you consider new opportunities.

- You might be reasonably skillful in four or five different things. Most of us have multiple capacities and interests, but what we want to establish is our superpower. What are you uniquely great at? Summarize that in one statement.

- If you know what you plan to say "Yes" to, it is far easier to decide what to say "No" to (this applies to every business and brand as well). Your awareness of your unique value eliminates much confusion in professional decision-making.

Most companies or managers prefer to hire through referrals. Algorithms won't hire you. You need to sell yourself to people using brain-friendly messaging tactics. Your main job is to equip others with brief value statements—memory darts—that sum up your unique value and make it easy to generate targeted referrals. People won't be able to remember five things. Give them the most important one.

You can use a similar format to the company brand positioning statement I described in the previous chapter to create a memorable personal/professional branding statement for an individual, as you explain your value to existing or potential employers:

"I provide (this specific capability and experience) to (this specific kind of employer) in order to (fix this pain/ meet this ongoing need) through my (differentiating superpower)."

Or, to summarize even further, use Mark Schaefer's template: "Only I _____" (fill in the blank with what you offer that is differentiated or unique).

For example, an IT leader might write: "I bring seven years of successful experience managing and growing teams of programmers in order to meet tight development deadlines for software companies that require high-touch collaborative leadership."

One hiring manager in a global company told Catherine Morgan that he spends no more than thirty seconds scanning a resume to see if something interesting pops out. Surprise: Generic jargon isn't interesting. If there's nothing remarkable, he's on to the next one. Even if you're well qualified, as Morgan puts it, you have to be right up-front with why your audience should care. It's not their job to figure you out, it's your job to communicate clearly and quickly.

Having a clear grasp of your professional identity is crucial throughout your career, but especially when you reenter the workforce after a downsizing or a protracted time out of the marketplace. During these times, people typically experience a lot of anxiety (and perhaps imposter syndrome), questioning their worth and their potential value to others.

Leadership executive Kari Gormley notes that we tend to focus on negativity during stressful times, and the brain's amygdala (which regulates emotion and memory) can become inflamed with fear and paralyzed with doubt.[57] We can easily fall into the vortex of believing negative stories, statements, and words that sabotage our confidence. That's when we need someone from the outside to speak fresh truth and counteract unhealthy thoughts. We need personal brand reinforcement.

I have consulted with dozens of talented people who have been in that discouraging place of transition. In fact, in my mid-20s, I went through an abrupt change of direction that left me feeling completely lost as a professional. I had no idea who I was or where I was going, or what value I could bring. I wish I had had a coach at that time who could have helped me rewrite my internal narratives by surfacing the positive strengths I did have.

As it turns out, clarity about your identity (the words that describe your unique strengths, skills, value, and experience) is crucial to navigating those difficult periods. Your perceived value is not determined by a current role, or by the reactions of others, but stands on its own despite any circumstances. You continue to possess specific value-adding attributes. You bring this kind of tangible contribution. You have success stories to share that highlight what we can do.

Internal clarity allows you to more confidently approach the marketplace with the same messages that you are telling yourself about your identity. You may need an outside perspective to attain it, and you certainly need much internal self-coaching to maintain it.

Know your enemy, and know yourself. Your personal brand is all about knowing yourself and sharing that (skillfully) with others.

CHAPTER 23:

Social Media

"Through an arbitrary problem, I had arrived
at a tenet of good writing: brevity wins."
—MICHAEL WINTER

I jumped into the social media scene early on. It turned my writing upside down.

Blogging helped me find my writing voice and develop my ideas about communication. But it was Twitter (with its initial 140-character limit) that forced me to learn how to distill. Compressing thoughts into small bits felt awkward at first, but the genius of short-form social media is that every creator had to learn to adjust to limited attention spans by practicing brevity.

In academia, I (and many others) had learned to be detailed and complete. Now we had to communicate in fragments. It's all about the snippets.

The discipline of focus is a major part of succeeding with social media. Focus in the sense of making your messages eminently digestible; but you also need to have a clear focus about who your audience is and what they will find valuable from you. "Spray and pray" is not a good formula for effective social media usage.

By and large, the whole point of most social media posts (written, video, or images) is to get right to the point. And if it's a longer article or video, it had better be up-front engaging, or no one will stick with it. Clarity wins in the quick-hit online world.

Clarity wins in the quick-hit online world.

Social media is a good training ground for creating RAS-friendly messaging, but there are dangers there as well. Here are a few points of wisdom based on years of hands-on experience:

- As a general rule, don't create long-winded dissertations on social platforms. Social media is built for short attention spans and skimming, not for long-form writing. Instead, seek to make a single point or share a single resource. You're making an impression, not providing an education.

- An accompanying visual to your post or article will generally increase interest level and engagement. You're seeking to entice an RAS that likes visual stimulation.

- Package your written message using brevity and shortcuts (not long, drawn-out text paragraphs) to create engagement on social media posts. For instance, if you are creating a longer article for a blog post, break it up with headers and bullet points.

- Be careful about wading into controversial topics when sharing on a public platform. Even innocuous-seeming comments can come back to bite you in our polarized environment. You might be correct in your own mind, but there's a massive pool of mental and emotional metadata out there. Political, social, technical, and philosophical commentary typically requires a good bit of explanation and nuance, which is not possible on social media sites.

- Choose your activity on social media platforms wisely. Be clear about your ROTI (Return On Time Investment). Be active where your target audience is most active and easily found (for me, on the professional side, that's LinkedIn). Not every platform provides the same value for every person.

- And always remember—the Internet never forgets. Take a deep breath, review, and maybe even delete that intended post that's going to step on inflamed toes. One ill-advised tweet or meme can ruin your reputation.

Have a clear purpose if you engage in social media. One of its best uses is to establish yourself as a thought leader by consistently sharing your insights and other resources around your particular area of interest. The drip-drip-drip of social media posts over time can create a solid and memorable impression of you in the minds of others, especially when you are generous and helpful with your expertise.

CLARITY SPOTLIGHT

Author, investor, and C-level business consigliere Carol Roth (a self-described "recovering investment banker"—great memory dart!) has made TV appearances for more than thirteen years, sharing sometimes provocative input on current events and business issues. Her expertise in delivering compelling sound bites is not confined to television, however. One of her Twitter exchanges in 2012 with TV host and friend Piers Morgan ended with an amusing six-word tweet (just Google the phrase, "right next to the word 'muskets'").

This "sound bite" was so powerful it became viral, led to an approximate 25 percent increase in followers for her account in the weeks that followed, and is still referenced regularly today, more than a decade later.[58]

As a seasoned writer, Carol recognizes that wrapping the briefest number of words around an idea is powerfully memorable, which she said is the same concept that underlies how slogans and jingles embed themselves in our minds. She noted that comedians workshop their jokes regularly in front of a live audience to figure out how to prune the material for maximum impact. "Prune for punchiness" would be a good slogan for every type of communicator.

CHAPTER 24:

Networking

"Becoming well known (at least among your prospects
& connections) is the most valuable element in the
connection process."

—JEFFREY GITOMER

When it comes to networking, Mark Zuckerberg, CEO of Meta Platforms, parent company of Facebook, put it this way: "People influence people. Nothing influences people more than a recommendation from a trusted friend. A trusted referral influences people more than the best broadcast message. A trusted referral is the Holy Grail of advertising."

People open doors and create new avenues of advancement far more effectively than algorithms do. But you have to provide the clarity about who you are and where you want to go, so that others know which doors to open.

One of my favorite things to do is help people become effective networkers. As a natural introvert, I struggled for years in social settings. I thought networking was equivalent to schmoozing, and I was not a fan of superficial small talk. So, like a lot of introverts, I'd tend to find one or two people to go deep with.

In settings large or small, however, I'd find that people really struggled to describe simply and clearly who they are and what they did. In a networking setting, where encounters are typically brief (at least initially), clarity of expression matters. Handing out a business card or mentioning a job title doesn't really get below the surface. So, I'd ask questions and try to get stories to the surface, because, well, I'm curious. And eventually the really interesting stuff would come out.

I'm still not great at schmoozing, but I love asking questions, analyzing, clarifying, and figuring people out. That's my style of networking. And once I listen to their stories, and perhaps help them sum up their purpose and value with clarity, I can pigeonhole them accurately in my memory. And I'm now in a unique position to do the most value-adding business practice of all: make referrals.

Your professional network is the source of your future opportunities. So, you need to equip your colleagues with clarity—the memorable words and images that best portray who you are.

- Don't jump into a networking opportunity by blabbing all about your needs or professional goals right away, which will tend to shut down the brain of your listener (remember: They are seeking a WIIFM). Be brief and succinct about yourself, while seeking to draw them out.

- Create warm and interesting relationships by being a "storyasker." Ask others about their role, their goals, their needs, their challenges, and so on. Sometimes, when introduced to someone new, I'll say, "So, give me your story…in less than sixty seconds." After stammering around for a few seconds, they'll mention several highlights, and that's all the fuel I need to continue asking more questions and keep the conversation going. People love to tell their stories. Focus on others and take interest.

- Be sure to prepare a few brief stories you can tell others that illustrate what value you bring and what types of open doors you are looking to find. Don't assume that people you meet will have a good idea of what you do and what a good business opportunity for you looks like. You need to plant that metadata and paint those pictures.

- Make it your goal to network to help others achieve their goals. And remember this: Many people are willing to help you if you just give them a simple, distilled understanding of your professional direction. If you're too generic, they can't refer you.
- Be sure to continue networking with your existing clients. They will be your best source of referrals, and believe it or not, they often have an incomplete or inaccurate view of your business value. Equip them with the words and stories that they can easily pass on to others.

> **Your professional network is the source of your future opportunities. So, you need to equip your colleagues with clarity—the memorable words and images that best portray who you are.**

For a deeper dive into the power and practices of referral networking, I'll close by recommending my book *Clarity Wins* for your perusal.

CLARITY SPOTLIGHT
—EVA DANIEL

After a couple decades in the communications industry and most recently as a senior speechwriter for Ramsey Solutions, Eva decided to launch her own public speech consulting company (The Speak Shop).[59]

One of her neighbors, who knew I enjoyed helping out new entrepreneurs and start-ups with positioning and branding, introduced us.

Over coffee (of course!) and on several virtual calls, we brainstormed her hopes and experiences and arrived at a distinguishing message and set of offerings, including a well-defined set of two potential target clients.

Eva had a lot of expertise and knowledge, but she experienced the challenge that so many other brilliant entrepreneurs have faced over the years—where to focus, and how to say it? This is actually a continuous challenge for many established businesses as well.

For Eva, one of the most helpful things was grasping the idea that customers buy templates, frameworks, and systems (specifics); and the sooner you can create those (and name them), the more quickly you will build your brand.

I had to go through the same process some years back; clients could see the value of clarity, but you can't buy that notion in the abstract. However, they knew how to buy *workshops*, so I marketed a suite of clarity workshops.

People want expertise, and they find it easier to buy that expertise packaged in specific and tangible offerings.

This book—which is really a practical handbook explaining how to use the clarity framework—is meant to give the broadest possible audience a host of immediate takeaways for the most common circumstances. You can apply these practices as an individual; but the greatest impact will be teams and companies that together embrace the approach and transform their organization. The Clarity Fuel Formula is long-overdue universal protocol for effective human-to-human communication, and is adaptable and applicable for just about any setting.

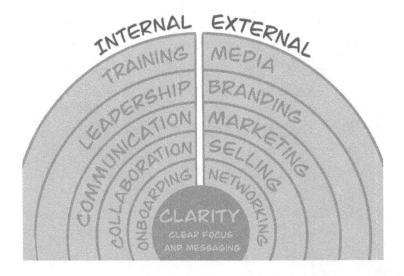

Microsoft recently surveyed 31,000 professionals in 31 countries and analyzed trillions of what they call "productivity signals" across the full suite of their Microsoft 365 product family (MS Office, Teams, OneDrive, Outlook, and other solutions).[60]

Their findings underscored the huge need for better communication practices when it comes to efficiency and productivity. Some data points included:

- The average employee spends 57% of their time communicating (in meetings, email, and chats) and 43% of their time creating (documents, spreadsheets, presentations).
- The number one productivity disruptor is inefficient meetings, followed closely (number three) by having too many meetings. Number two? Lack of clear goals.
- 55% reported that next steps at the end of meetings are unclear, and 56% indicated that it is hard to summarize what happens.

Moving the productivity needle using better communication techniques such as those in the Clarity Fuel Formula can lead to improved employee satisfaction and significant cost savings, particularly when implemented across an enterprise.

Every type of industry and organization—large or small—can benefit from targeted applications of the clarity framework. And every one of the practices we've briefly touched on in this book can be expanded upon and applied in a series of workshops based on applying clarity to any organization's workflow particular needs. See the Appendix to learn more about the clarity workshops the author provides.

Now you know the rules. And you have the tools. The fact is, every single person, and every single role or profession (with the possible exception of monks under a lifelong vow of silence) will benefit from simpler, clearer communications. You'll spend the rest of your life practicing what you're learned in this book, and everyone you interact with will appreciate it.

You're ready to win the noisy battle. Let's get to the point, shall we? Let's do clarity!

ACKNOWLEDGMENTS

I'd like to express my heartfelt appreciation to those who have supported this effort over many years:

- My middle Tennessee encouragers, including folks who gather at High Brow Coffee, Elroy Coffee Co., Christ Community Church, and the Westhaven Men's Hangout group (the donut church).
- Dozens of fellow consultants, speakers, and thought leaders who have so generously provided valuable feedback as my thinking about clarity has evolved.
- The members and leaders of LTEN (Life Sciences Trainers & Educators Network), who have helped shape the Clarity Fuel Formula through numerous professional workshop engagements.
- Josh Bernoff, expert editor and author coach extraordinaire.
- The Morgan James Publishing team, who believed in the clarity message and provided skillful guidance throughout the complex process of getting it into print.

- Above all: El Roi, the God who sees me, shepherds me, and provides the most abundant and enduring examples of clarity principles and practices. All of this, and all of me, is Yours.

Clarity Resources

I've facilitated clarity workshops for my many clients over the years in just about every possible format. These sessions can be live or virtual, small or large group, local or global, shorter sessions or multiday engagements.

The goal is always the same: immediate, enduring, high-impact skill development.

To learn more about how clarity keynotes and workshops can get you and your team to the next level of communication excellence, visit: www.clarityfuelworkshops.com.

I've been very glad that there are many other people who have contributed to the clarity discussion over the years/decades/millennia. I'm one of many voices trying to bring simplicity and sense to our noisy world.

Sharing these many resources is easier online, where I can easily update the list and immediately provide links.

So, I'd invite you to peruse my recommended books, experts, articles, and other resources online at: www.thepointbook.info.

For those who wish to delve deeper into the specific references contained in this book, there will be active links to all those articles and books on that page also.

My prior book, *Clarity Wins*, is available on Amazon. Here's a shortcut link: www.claritywins.org.

ABOUT THE AUTHOR

Steve Woodruff is on a mission to help others practice effective communication. The interplay of ideas, words, and people have always fascinated him. Someone once told him, "You didn't find clarity…clarity found you."

Over more than four decades, Steve has taught, sold, presented, preached, marketed, blogged, authored, collaborated, coached, networked… and at the core of every one of those activities is figuring out how to communicate clearly and effectively. That's how the idea of finding a single, practical recipe—the Clarity Fuel Formula—evolved.

Steve is a graduate of Vanderbilt University and has a long history of business-building in healthcare and life sciences as a consultant, trainer, and speaker. He released his first book (*Clarity Wins*) with a focus on helping professionals with their branding and referral networking. He has since conducted numerous workshops on communications clarity for a variety of local and global audiences.

Steve's favorite activity is consulting with individuals to find their professional purpose through individual and group brainstorming sessions. This is followed closely by firepit time with family, friends, books, and libations.

He and his wife Sandy both hail originally from Connecticut. They have five grown sons and live in the historic city of Franklin, Tennessee.

ENDNOTES

1 "Builders demolish Russian oligarch's French chateau," *BBC* website, December 5, 2012

2 Current World Population," worldometer website.

3 "2023 The State of Business Communication," Grammarly Business website

4 Manuel Noriega's Favorite Playlist," Agent Bill Wilson, YouTube playlist, last updated March 9, 2021.

5 Mark Schaeffer, "Content Shock: Why content marketing is not a sustainable strategy," Businesses Grow blog

6 Rebecca Moody, "Screen Time Statistics: Average Screen Time in US vs. the rest of the world," comparitech website, updated March 15, 2023

7 Jack Flynn, "35+ Amazing Advertising Statistics [2023]: Data + Trends," Zippia website, January 16, 2023

8 Jack Flynn, "20 Incredible Productivity Statistics [2023]: Average Employee Productivity in the U.S.," Zippia website, November 2, 2022

9 "Volatility, uncertainty, complexity and ambiguity," Wikipedia

10   Josh Bernoff, personal interview

11   Ann Latham, *The Power of Clarity* (London: Bloomsbury Business publishing, 2021), Edition 1, p. 7

12   Brian Fugere, Chelsea Hardaway, Jon Warshawsky, *Why Business People Speak Like Idiots: A Bullfighter's Guide* (New York, NY: Free Press, 2005), Edition 1

13   George Markowsky, "Physiology," Britannica website

14   "Reticular formation," Wikipedia

15   "Reticular Activating System: Definition & Function," Study dot com website

16   Milo O. Frank, *How to Get Your Point Across in 30 Seconds or Less* (Gallery Books, reissue edition April 15, 1990), p. 14.

17   Michael W. Richardson, "How Much Energy Does the Brain Use?" BrainFacts on-line, February 1, 2019

18   Daniel Levitin, *The Organized Mind* (New York, NY: Plume, division of Penguin Random House, 2014), Edition 1

19   Jack Appleman, personal interview

20   Thomas Clifford, personal interview

21   Kevin and Jackie Freiberg, "20 Reasons Why Herb Kelleher Was One Of The Most Beloved Leaders Of Our Time," *Forbes*, January 4, 2019

22   Barbara Minto, *The Pyramid Principle: Logic in Writing and Thinking* (London: FT Publishing International, 2021) Edition 3

23   Catherine Morgan, *This Isn't Working! Evolving the Way We Work to Decrease Stress, Anxiety, and Depression* (Pensacola, FL: Indigo River Publishing, 2023), Edition 1

24 Jim VandeHei, Mike Allen, Roy Schwartz, *Smart Brevity—the Power of Saying More with Less* (New York, NY: Workman Publishing, 2022), Edition 1, p. 2

25 David Rock, *Your Brain at Work* (New York, NY: HarperCollins Publishers, 2009), Edition 1, p. 25

26 Josh Bernoff, "Bad Writing Costs Businesses Billions," *Daily Beast*, updated April 13, 2017

27 Donald Davidson, PhD, personal interview

28 Bob Goff, *Live in Grace, Walk in Love* (Nashville, TN: Thomas Nelson Books, 2019), Edition 1, p. 385

29 Steve Woodruff, "Successfully Partnering with Suppliers," *LTEN Focus*, summer 2017 Edition

30 Blue Spoon Consulting website

31 Kim Catania, personal interview

32 Steph Dreyer, personal interview

33 Alison Quinn, personal interview

34 Chip Heath and Dan Heath, *Made to Stick: Why Some Ideas Survive and Others Die* (New York, NY: Random House Publishing Group, 2007), Edition 1, p. 110

35 Chris Kolmar, "75 Incredible Email Statistics [2023]: How Many Emails Are Sent Per Day?" Zippia website, March 30, 2023

36 *Smart Brevity: The Power of Saying More with Less, Axios and Gallup Communications Study*, Axios and Gallup

37 Janice Tomich, "80% of Presentations Fail — Do Yours?" Janice Tomich website

38 Guy Kawasaki, "The 10/20/30 Rule of PowerPoint," October 24, 2016, Guy Kawasaki website

39 Michael Stelzner, personal interview

40   Tom Martin, personal interview

41   David Davis, personal interview

42   Gallup (Marcus Buckingham and Donald Clifton), *Now, Discover Your Strengths: The revolutionary Gallup program that shows you how to develop your unique talents and strengths* (Washington, DC: Gallup Press, 2020)

43   Jennifer Muscik, personal interview

44   John Novello, personal interview

45   Jeffrey Taylor, personal interview

46   Steve Haase, personal interview

47   Simon Sinek, *Start With Why: How Great Leaders Inspire Everyone to Take Action* (New York, NY: Penguin Books, 2009) Edition 1

48   "Our Purpose," Edward Jones website

49   "Purpose & Values," M&T Bank website

50   "Investor Relations," Harley-Davidson website

51   "About us" charity: water website

52   "About us" Sodexo website

53   Steve Woodruff and Jason Zeman, "Branding the Training Department at Valeant," *LTEN Focus*, winter 2016 Edition

54   Steve Woodruff, Clarity Wins (Franklin, TN: ClarityFuel Publishing, 2018), Edition 1, available on Amazon

55   Romar Learning Solutions website

56   Mark Schaefer, *The Content Code* (Schaefer Marketing Solutions, 2015), Edition 1

57   Kari Gormley, personal interview

58   Carol Roth, personal interview

59   The Speak Shop website

60 Microsoft Worklab, Work Trend Index Annual Report, "Will AI Fix Work?"

A free ebook edition is available with the purchase of this book.

To claim your free ebook edition:

1. Visit MorganJamesBOGO.com
2. Sign your name CLEARLY in the space
3. Complete the form and submit a photo of the entire copyright page
4. You or your friend can download the ebook to your preferred device

A **FREE** ebook edition is available for you or a friend with the purchase of this print book.

CLEARLY SIGN YOUR NAME ABOVE

Instructions to claim your free ebook edition:
1. Visit MorganJamesBOGO.com
2. Sign your name CLEARLY in the space above
3. Complete the form and submit a photo of this entire page
4. You or your friend can download the ebook to your preferred device

Print & Digital Together Forever.

Snap a photo

Free ebook

Read anywhere

Printed in the USA
CPSIA information can be obtained
at www.ICGtesting.com
JSHW021920220923
49004JS00002B/12

9 781636 982380